Andrey Mir

The Viral Inquisitor

and other essays on postjournalism and media ecology

ISBN 978-1-7773589-3-8

Toronto, Canada

Table of contents

Our guide through the media labyrinth. Foreword by Martin Gurri

Andrey Mir is the most profound observer of media, traditional and digital, writing today. No one else comes close. Mir is our present-day version of Marshall McLuhan – whose disciple, not coincidentally, he is – only without McLuhan's self-importance and opacity. Mir writes in Toronto, Canada, McLuhan's city. From there, he has delivered an astonishing series of books and articles that have changed our understanding of how the structures of communication have influenced history – and how they will shape the future.

Humans are word-obsessed animals. We closely scrutinize media content: Is it true or false? Good or evil? From a famous author or a mere unknown? Yet the truly powerful effects are produced by media ***structure***, the form a medium imposes on communication. The structure of information is the environment, the landscape, on which not only our intellectual lives but our social relations evolve. Mass communication facilitated a society based on top-down control, for example, while the internet – Mir calls it "the emancipation of authorship" – has famously disrupted hierarchical arrangements. This, of course, is what McLuhan meant by his enigmatic formula, "The medium is the message."

Mir is the foremost practitioner today of the environmental approach to understanding media. Which is another way of saying: he thinks big. In the essays collected for this book, the reader will encounter a set of capacious and highly original concepts that will serve as guide through the twisting labyrinth of modern media.

Let me offer a small sample.

A ***viral editor***, Mir observes, governs accuracy on the web. Complaining about the huge volume of online lies is a commonplace ritual these days – but we only know these lies exist because they have been exposed as such by the web itself. (The viral editor belonged to the early phase of the digital era. In our politically turbulent present, the unmasking of falsehood has been undertaken by a ***viral inquisitor***.)

Postjournalism is what happened to newspapers after their 20th-century business model, based on advertisement, collapsed. One may think that the New York Times has become heavily biased on behalf of progressive politics, but that's only superficially true. The Times has effectively commoditized political polarization as its new business model. To make up for lost advertisement, it now makes a profit by becoming a sheltered garden for readers of a particular persuasion.

The historical transition from oral to textual communication was accompanied by tremendous psychological changes: for example, memory was no longer of supreme importance and emotive poetic language made less sense than logical prose. Mir maintains that the prevalence of the web has inaugurated an era of ***digital orality***, "a new hybrid state of mind" that will alter the way we perceive the world – for example, by changing the parameters of shared truth. ("Two plus two is doubted if said by Hitler," Mir notes, only half in jest.)

Everything Mir writes is original, his prose sparkles with aphorisms. His ideas, as I said, are immense and counterintuitive, but they are persuasive and easily understood. His knowledge of the history of media is astounding – I know a bit about this subject, and I invariably learn from him. His fearless speculation on a future driven by artificial intelligence is mind-expanding and resembles the best of science fiction.

We need explainers of Mir's scope and breadth of vision. Contemporary humanity is a child lost in the woods, haunted by riddles at every turn. How did we get here? Where are we headed? Amid the affluence and luxury, given global communication and cheap travel to iconic places, what is the right path for us as individuals and as a people – and why? Yet authors today spew endless amounts of content, textual and visual, on frivolous subjects – celebrity, identity, the latest uproar surrounding Donald Trump.

Mir transcends the fractured triviality of our day and stands in closer alignment with the towering sages of the last century. He should be compared to Oswald Spengler, José Ortega y Gasset, Arnold Toynbee, no less than to McLuhan – thinkers who framed the human story in the widest possible context, thereby enlarging our understanding of the present and casting a flickering light into possible futures. Those writers may have been right or wrong, but they painted on a huge canvas and invited us to think of ourselves on a similar scale.

So it is with Andrey Mir. The ideas you are about to discover in the essays that follow are adventurous and imaginative – and, if I may say so, they redeem our age.

Martin Gurri

Preface by the author

Many people feel like an era is coming to an end, and they are right. It is not just political and cultural disturbances that underlie the latest and upcoming turmoil – the political and cultural changes themselves are media effects. The world is switching from print to digital. Media are the hardware of society, and culture is its software; a change in hardware makes all habitual software obsolete and disrupts the previous balances in human conditions.

The essays in this collection explore the tectonic media shift from print to digital, which I believe is at the core of all contemporary political and cultural upheavals. Digital media have been forming an environment in which more and more human activities now reside. To reveal how the shift from print to digital affects culture and society, the essays employ several key concepts.

The instrumental and environmental views of media represent two ways of understanding media. The instrumental approach implies that media are used as tools for achieving certain outcomes. This approach tends to focus on the intentions of the user and the efficiency of the medium. Unlike the instrumental approach, which looks at what we do with media, the environmental approach is concerned with what media do to us. By affecting us and our interactions with everything else, media have become a terraforming force. The environmental power of a medium is the primary focus of media ecology, as introduced by McLuhan in his famous "The medium is the message."

The emancipation of authorship by the Internet describes the explosion of people's access not just to information but, most importantly, to self-expression. Before the Internet, humankind had around 300 million authors in its entire history. After the introduction of the Internet, in a mere 40 years, this number has jumped to almost 5 billion. All these people have acquired the technical capacity to convey whatever they want far beyond their physical reach. This has caused profound changes in society.

The blogosphere and social media have encouraged everyone to share their opinions and attitudes, regardless of how prepared and well thought out they are. Next, digital platforms facilitate people's engagement in every possible way and even automate it with buttons such as "share" and "like", while algorithms harvest users' reactions. People's reactions to content and each other are the most valuable assets of both users' personal social capital and platforms' digital capital.

These environmental settings, fostered by digital media, make society incredibly agitated. Presenting oneself to others to elicit reactions in order to gain social capital redirects the focus of ethics from ***doing*** to ***being*** – from merits to identities. This affects all human interactions and institutions, including news media, governments, corporations, education, and even personal relationships.

Heavy and lazy authors comprise two factions of emancipated authorship. Heavy authors contribute content – posts and comments. Lazy authors contribute their reactions in various digital forms: by sharing, liking, or even viewing. Their reactions are selective and therefore meaningful – they select content for distribution.

Given their tremendous numbers, lazy authors are the ones who keep the entire machine rolling. Their activity is registered and converted into labor by algorithms, making lazy authorship the main asset of digital capitalism (in contrast to heavy authors – the producers of content and gatekeepers of social significance, who were an asset of industrial capitalism in the print era).

The Viral Editor is a dispersed mechanism of content selection and distribution, a neural network whose processing chips are users. When users see something noteworthy, they share it in the hope of receiving a response and gaining social capital. They want to affect others. If others deem it worthy, they share, like, and comment, too. Each one selects, edits, or adds something in the process of viral distribution, which is why it is called the Viral Editor. Through the collective work of selection and distribution, the Viral Editor turns the noteworthy for one into the newsworthy for many, thus killing traditional journalism.

In the blogosphere, the Viral Editor was solely human driven. Social media introduced automation into the Viral Editor, enabling it to extract not just opinions but also attitudes, thereby expanding the forms and volume of users' engagement. With this transformation, the Viral Editor has mutated into the **Viral Inquisitor** (a metaphor suggested by Martin Gurri at a workshop we attended at the University of British Columbia in 2022). The Viral Inquisitor delivers attitudes, not just content, to whom it may agitate the most, leading people to watch each other's reactions and thus creating a new, dispersed, and all-pervading embodiment of the Big Brother who always watches you.

Postjournalism describes the state of journalism after the news media switched from being generously paid by advertising to desperately seeking digital subscriptions. This change in the business model was caused by the Internet, which took away ad money. It happened simultaneously around the world in the early 2010s. As a last resort, the media all rushed in on "Digital First!", seeking subscriptions, or rather affirmation, from the early digital adopters – mostly young, progressive, educated urbanites. The media started chasing this audience and adopted its values, having abandoned news coverage for the broader population.

The issue was that, because of the Viral Editor, the digital public did not consume news from the media anyway. The digital public always already know all the relevant news from the news feed. However, when something disturbing happens, people want to validate the significance of disturbing news through authorized sources. This led the news media to switch from news supply to news validation, having become not news dealers but news notaries.

Early in this new pursuit, the media learned to validate the significance of disturbing news within the value systems of their new and quite narrow referential group. But eventually, they began prioritizing news that required value validation and applied these value guidelines to covering everything. Trump aided in this and even made a few news outlets great again, which only forced the rest of them to follow suit and reject the principles of old journalism.

Thus, sometime around 2018, the mutation of journalism into postjournalism had been completed. If journalism claimed to portray the world as-it-is, postjournalism imposes the world as-it-should-be.

The Digital Rush was a cultural movement of the early 2010s, when traditional institutions, led by the news media, rushed to adopt digital technologies and, therefore, digital culture. They targeted the leading digital demographics at the time, the digital progressives, and embraced their ethos along the way.

The process itself is not unique: any medium empowers its early adopters and imposes their values on the rest of society. A new culture always rides the wave of new technologies. This time, however, due to the instant proliferation of the new dominant medium, it took just a decade, not centuries, and the aging of the early new-media adopters could not mitigate their disruptive and oftentimes nihilistic aptitude typical of the youth, normally marginal to the establishment.

The young and progressive digital visionaries of Silicon Valley provided the hardware for societal changes, while the young and progressive discursive elites, among the first to digitize, introduced their cultural software into all societal practices – from politics and education to pop culture, journalism, and corporate standards. Technology always comes with an ideology; this is how it happened this time. Society has submitted to the new values, propelling their source, the digital progressives, from activist marginalia to the establishment. Such was the immediate effect of the Digital Rush of the early 2010s.

Soon, however, reactionary backlash and nostalgic ressentiment fired back. Excluded from the mainstream agenda, the older, less urban, less educated, and less progressive demographics reached the critical mass of social media use sometime by the mid-2010s. Much like their younger and more progressive predecessors 5–7 years before, they became able to communicate to each other their indignation regarding the establishment, now captured by progressive ideas. This indignation, triggered by the mainstream media and amplified by social media, turned into a political demand and led to Brexit, Trump, and all the subsequent waves of right-wing reactions. The conservative backlash of the late 2010s was the secondary, recoil effect of the Digital Rush of the early 2010s.

The sum result was soaring polarization. Political and cultural struggles have moved onto the new media hardware and embraced its settings. Since the main effect of digital media, particularly social media platforms, has been to catalyze self-expression, the cultural, political, and economic significance of identity claims has skyrocketed.

Can a new balance between polarized opposites be restored? It might, but the new balance, if ever established, will be very dynamic. In a print-based culture, the known was separated from the knower and detached into objective truth; this made the print-backed social equilibrium based on a heavy center. In digital conditions, truth belongs to anyone who claims it; therefore, social equilibrium, if ever achieved, can only be a balance between the heavy margins, which makes it highly volatile.

The acceleration of historical time can be explained as an increase in the number of events per period. Human history is shaped by media evolution, with the periods of certain media's domination getting shorter. Oral communication lasted tens of thousands of years, writing existed for five millennia, printing spanned for five centuries, electronic media has been around for a century and a half, and digital media emerged roughly three decades ago.

At some point in this progression, the duration of a media era became shorter than the lifespan of a generation. This generation can be called the **pivotal generation:** the people of that generation lived in more than one media epoch, and this happened for the first time in history. For most countries, the pivotal generation lived in the late 20th century. Their lives encompassed both industrial and post-industrial eras (in many countries, the pivotal generation spanned into three eras: agrarian, industrial and post-industrial). After the pivotal generation, technological eras come faster than the changing of generations, leaving society with no time to adapt.

The shrinking durations of eras, when put in a row, create a clear countdown pattern: "10, 9, 8, 7...". We are living somewhere near the count of "one." On the count of "zero," the ultimate historical event will happen. What will this event be? I trust the reader to answer this question after finishing the book.

Digital orality describes the state of the mind and culture induced by the use of digital speech. Digital speech combines the features of writing and oral conversation. Similar to writing, digital speech is produced mostly by typing letters in the privacy of personal devices. Similar to oral utterances, digital speech represents the instant exchange of reactions, favoring emotional responses over elaborate reasoning. Digital speech is impulsive but not evanescent: it can be recorded and delivered beyond the circle of immediate interlocutors, leading them to seek affirmation not just from each other but from a larger audience and thus expanding identity signalling into the public exhibition.

Because of this oral-written hybridization, digital orality reverses the effects of literacy and retrieves the effects of orality. The imperceptible but profound cognitive and cultural effect of typing-and-taping results in shaping new tribal conditions, now based not on the primary orality of preliterate cultures but on the digital orality of post-literate culture.

These and other concepts are applied in the essays of this collection to analyze various practical and theoretical aspects – ranging from the competition between CNN and Fox News, the postjournalism of generative AI, and platforms enslaving users while serving them, to political polarization, the shifting epistemology of truth, and the impacts of screens on children.

Most of the essays of this collection were published in Discourse and City Journal. I want to express my sincere gratitude to the editors: David Masci, Christina Behe, and Jennifer Tiedemann (Discourse) and Brian Anderson, Paul Beston, and Theodore Kupfer (City Journal).

I am especially grateful to people who have influenced many insights in these essays: Martin Gurri, author of *The Revolt of the Public*, and Robert Logan, author of *The Alphabet Effect* (among many other books on media) and co-author of Marshall McLuhan. As the reader may notice, I refer to them the most after McLuhan himself.

A.M.
Toronto – Cape Cod,
July 2024.

The Viral Inquisitor

Social media have unleashed a culture of instant judging[1]

In the beginning was the Viral Editor

The phrase "random act of journalism," first appearing in the early 2000s, described the willingness of bloggers to report news.[2] Mass coverage of big and small events by ordinary people was, as the media analyst Mathew Ingram put it, "what happens when journalism is everywhere."[3] The Internet emancipated authorship, and people started to share what they witnessed or thought, looking to gain a response and recognition. Such "citizen journalism" deprived the professional media of its monopoly over news coverage, enabling alternative agenda-setting and causing what analyst Martin Gurri calls the "crisis of authority"[4] that spurred a wave of global unrest.

But reporting seems an insufficient description of this kind of mass online activity. After all, people don't just report on events that they have witnessed. They also select, process, emphasize, illustrate, write headlines, and decide how to present information. Basically, they do the job of an editor. The Internet combines and reinforces their editorial efforts. As a result, Internet users perform a collective version of the editorial work that once took place in newsrooms. If professional editors serve as gatekeepers, determining the importance of various stories ***before*** publication, the Internet opens the gates, deciding on the significance of content ***after*** it's published, in the process of viral distribution. Hence, it's not just a

---

[1] The essay is based on the article with the same title in *City Journal*. (2023, Spring). Revised for book publication.

[2] Lasica, Joseph D. (2003, March 12). "Random acts of journalism." *Inside social media*.

[3] Ingram, Mathew. (2011, November 18). "What happens when journalism is everywhere?" *GigaOm*.

[4] Gurri, Martin. (2018 [2014]). *The Revolt of the Public and the Crisis of Authority in the New Millennium*.

collective editor – it's what I call the Viral Editor.[1] Anyone can post anything, including rubbish. But people then vote with their likes, reposts, and comments, thereby distributing content according to what they find interesting. The Viral Editor does not just provide the selection, framing, and distribution of content; it is also a nonstop referendum that decides what is important.

The Viral Editor appears to offer numerous advantages over traditional professional media. First, it can marshal evidence from anywhere. News organizations must dispatch reporters to cover a faraway event, but people with cell phones will already be there, on the ground. Second, it possesses more expertise than any single newsroom ever could. It recruits all the experts and witnesses that society has, and they all compete for recognition by sharing their knowledge. Third, the Viral Editor can deliver the news precisely to whom it may concern. Our news feed is made by our friends – people with similar tastes, interests, views, and socioeconomic statuses. They – we – select, comment, and deliver to one another information with the highest possible relevance not just for "people like us" but precisely for us.

Finally, the fact-checking capacity of the Viral Editor exceeds that of any professional institution. If a lie is important, it will spread until it reaches those who can debunk it, and they will do so for the sake of response and recognition. A rebuttal may not reverse the impact of the initial lie, but it will be present for those willing to see. If a lie is not important, it simply will not be distributed.

With these attributes, the Viral Editor seemed to have the capacity to improve conversations, content, and even the participants themselves. Regardless of all the nonsense and filth posted online, people generally want to put their better selves forward. The mechanism had the potential to improve everything it touched.

From the Viral Editor to the algorithms of relevance

Alas, that's not how things have unfolded. That analysis of the Viral Editor may have seemed plausible in the era of the blogosphere, when

---

[1] The concept of the Viral Editor was first introduced in 2009. In English: *Human as Media. The Emancipation of Authorship*. (2014).

citizen journalism still dominated digital engagement. But with the rise of social-media platforms came a different and automated mechanism for determining relevance: algorithms.

The Viral Editor, a human-based mechanism of relevance, structured the blogosphere of the 2000s. Blogs followed the old rules of literature and journalism. Essentially the last texts of the Gutenberg era, many blog posts ran a few hundred words, requiring creative effort and logical organization on the part of the writer. They were also distributed by humans. Users themselves shared the links to blog posts they liked. Other users could see an important blog post only if they followed the blog or if their friends delivered it to them. Reading a post was always and everywhere a human decision, made with no algorithmic involvement. Comments and reposts rendered certain blog posts popular, thereby authorizing their significance.

If the number of journalists in the history of the news media can be estimated roughly at 1 million, the blogosphere era saw tens of millions of people enter the fray. By 2014, Tumblr was hosting 172 million blogs, and WordPress another 75 million. But the ecosystem had already changed. If the 2000s were the decade of the blogosphere, the 2010s became the decade of social media. The blogosphere continued to exist, but bloggers started using social-media platforms for distributing their blog content. In 2010, according to a survey by Technorati, 78 percent of bloggers used Twitter and 87 percent used Facebook.

The blogosphere was run by humans; social media are run by algorithms. The transition from human to algorithmic mechanisms of relevance unfolded in an instant. And it coincided with an explosion in authorship: while the number of bloggers reached a few hundred million, the number of social-media users has now hit 4.7 billion – more than half of humankind.

This transition changed the nature of digital engagement. The personal connection that users feel with their social-media contacts still matters. But as tech companies adapt to new economic realities and compete for scarce attention, algorithms increasingly determine the content to which a user is exposed.

Algorithms seek our engagement to collect our personal data and to get us to spend more time on a platform. While the Viral Editor could not be interfered with, algorithms, the intellectual property of corporations, can be artificially tuned. They have repurposed personal content customization from content delivery to advertising delivery. "The seemingly God-like abilities offered by the net were productized," wrote media theorist Douglas Rushkoff in 2019. "The Internet went from town hall to shopping mall."[1]

Indeed, just a decade after the Viral Editor seized the agenda-setting monopoly from the professional media, it lost it to the algorithms. The shift from the blogosphere to social media transformed the way people exchange information online. The transition was not only from Blogger and LiveJournal to Facebook and Twitter but also from slow blogging to fast digital exchange.

The implosion of the world into the user

At the most fundamental level, blogs were written text. A blog post was a personal diary entry, and writing one took time. It delayed individuals' reactions to events. This delay of reaction was a crucial factor. As the Soviet paleoanthropologist Boris Porshnev once noted, thought and speech require the inhibition of natural reflexes. The need to formulate thoughts and sentences mediates our gut reactions. This makes humans slowpokes compared with animals, but it also facilitates deliberation and cooperation, conferring evolutionary benefits. Writing became the highest form of this reaction delay: a literate culture may delay its response to events for days, months, or years, but the deliberation and cooperation that literacy engenders have allowed humans as a species to thrive and transform the planet and even near space into the Noosphere, the ecological niche of our species.

Social media have reversed this process. Seeking to extract more of their users' time and engagement, social-media platforms have made digital reactions almost as instantaneous as physiological reflexes. The Internet completed the transfer of our reactions into virtual space, reducing the transaction costs for sharing them with others.

Global cooperation of humans was an effect of literacy because literacy allowed us to communicate over time and space. But shouldn't social media make society even more cooperative? After all, people can now get more

---

[1] Rushkoff, Douglas. (2019, November 14). "Was Humanity Simply Not Ready for the Internet? A 1990s cyber enthusiast considers whether he's to blame for our digital woes". *Medium*.

responses to one another's thoughts than ever before. But the nature of human cooperation has changed dramatically. Lacking the deliberative element that writing requires, social-media posts often feature nothing but gut, emotive reactions.

The response of others is a currency needed to gain and maintain social status. Social media automatized response through the buttons of "like" and "share" and thus drastically reduced the effort needed to gain or give a response. The exchange of responses accelerated and made it possible to get a response with almost no content production (by posting a selfie, say). Increasingly, what the Viral Editor now selects and delivers to users is not content but other users.

The Internet completely removed the time-space restrictions on personal conversation. In physical reality, only those physically present could count on the reaction of their interlocutors. Communication in larger groups required mediation, procedures, or broadcasting. Only mediated communication could overcome the time-space restrictions of personal gathering and enable cooperation in bigger numbers. Social media dismiss these limitations of physical presence. When posting something online, a user can hope for a response from an unlimited number of others. However, all others, and all at once, want the same from this single user.

Media theorist Marshall McLuhan held that mechanical technologies extended each person's reach to the external environment, thus "exploding" the world for humans. Yet the advent of electricity, McLuhan suggested, "contracted" the world for everyone in a massive "implosion." "Our central nervous system is technologically extended to involve us in the whole of mankind and to incorporate the whole of mankind in us," wrote McLuhan.[1]

Though we can reach out to other people, other people can also reach out to us. Every social-media user is bombarded by everyone else's existential demands, thoroughly customized by algorithms to grab our attention. Friends, friends of friends, and strangers fill our news feed with their worldviews and expect immediate recognition of their rightness in exchange. "Our technology has enabled us to put all of our senses outside ourselves, with the result that we find our neighbor is inside, and not 'out there' any longer. When the senses go outside, not only Big Brother but

[1] McLuhan, Marshall. (1964). *Understanding Media. The Extensions of Man.* P. 4.

little brother goes inside," said McLuhan in the era of television, as if he foresaw the effect of social media.[1]

The birth of the Viral Inquisitor

Digital media not only compressed the time and space that once separated people but also enabled a new language: digital speech, which has traits of both oral and written communication. Like oral speech, it permits the instant exchange of replies; like writing, it leaves behind a record and can be transmitted in time and space. These features mean that people's spontaneous and mostly emotive efforts to establish their social statuses in conversation are no longer transient. The reactions of millions of people are accumulated, spread, and displayed to everyone else.

This new type of conversation, digital orality, has its benefits. It allows socialization at an unprecedented pace and scale. The Viral Editor still delivers the most relevant information to everyone. However, the ease of exchanging digital speech has shifted the focus of mass communication from reflections to reflexes, from substance to attitude. Social media demand that everyone relate to others, to their ideas, to their troubles and achievements – indeed, to their very existence.

Social media increasingly serve not to facilitate the simple exchange of written information but to sort out everyone's attitude toward the most pressing issues of the day. The wrong response to someone's hard-fought truth is punished by reciprocal aggression and various forms of ostracism.

Under these environmental conditions, affected by the algorithms and instantaneous exchange of digital reflexes, the Viral Editor morphed into the Viral Inquisitor, as Martin Gurri suggested to call it at a recent workshop. If the Viral Editor required from everyone participation in content selection, the Viral Inquisitor demands from everyone solidarity with the most widely held views of others.

The Viral Inquisitor is a relentless tormentor. British anthropologist Robin Dunbar famously hypothesized that the human brain can maintain stable social relationships with 120 to 150 individuals, the size of a tribal

---

[1] McLuhan, Marshall. (1962). "8 mm in context: the modern media and externalized senses," Dinner Address to the 1961 Conference on 8 mm Sound Film and Education at the Teachers College, Columbia University. In Louis Forsdale (Ed.), *The Proceedings of the Conference*, 1962, p. 21.

group or a village. Social media override Dunbar's number, burdening users with connections more numerous than what we can handle. Excessive social connections make people feel impelled to know hundreds of strangers, whose digital existence intrudes upon their personal space – their screens.

Through the same mechanisms that the Viral Editor used to customize content for everyone, the Viral Inquisitor gathers identity signals of others and delivers them precisely to those most likely to react. You may choose not to react, but when you eventually or accidentally react with a click, or even a longer pause in scrolling down, you fall into a trap of further customization and better-customized identity signalling. Sophisticated algorithms ensure that the Viral Inquisitor notes everyone's inclinations and preferences. The user can't escape from being exposed to the identity signals of others and their persisting demands for affirmation. If you react wrongly, you are guilty.

This makes the Viral Inquisitor a much more effective warden than the notorious Big Brother. The sins and thoughtcrimes of everyone get delivered precisely to those who can be alarmed and enraged. No KGB is capable of such all-pervasive control over everyone's wrongdoings and wrongthink. The Viral Inquisitor is the collective high priest of cancel culture.

The digital inquisition of truth

But perhaps the worst element of this transformation is the way it abets the emergence of post-truth. A persistent interrogator, the Viral Inquisitor extracts users' testimonies and checks them against the truths held by others. The Viral Inquisitor changes the way propositions are verified, challenging our very epistemology of truth.

Before literacy, a truth was confirmed by how well it comported with nature and its divine moving forces. Polytheism was the natural science of oral culture. To deal with nature, gods, and one another, humans made respective arrangements with all these. Better arrangements lasted longer and conferred better benefits on their participants – practice was the criterion of truth, to quote Marx with his materialism. Preliterate truths were conditional; they were negotiated and tested by outcomes.

Literacy separated truth from practice. It became possible to inscribe truth, to carry it on through time and space, amplifying its sacred meaning until it gained the status of the ultimate law. The so-called alphabet effect,[1] according to physicist and media theorist Robert K. Logan, went further. The linear code of abstract signs for meaningless sounds enabled abstract logic, monotheism, and the concept of absolute truth. The multitude of practical truths held by varying groups in various situations was replaced by one moral law: that of God. The truth inscribed in the Book was unified. In different times, the Book was the scripture, the code of laws, the textbook; all contained absolute truth. In written culture, truth belongs to nobody but solely to the highest authority and can only be interpreted.

In the same way that digital speech combines oral and written speech, digital orality combines the preliterate and literate epistemologies of truth. The emancipation of authorship by the Internet undermined preexisting authorities, including the authority of absolute truth. As millions of people entered the business of meaning-production, the broadcasting of absolute truth lost its monopoly. Scriptures and textbooks forfeited their power. The caste of priest-interpreters was replaced by multiple crowd-sourced interpretations of the world. People now vote for truth with clicks. Truth is again up for negotiation.

In the digital world, the truth of a given statement can be confirmed – again – by the practical outcomes that it generates. But these practical outcomes now happen in digital, not physical, reality. Since digital reality presents the world through the views of others, the truth of everyone is defined by the truths of others. Social media have legitimized crowd-sourced truths as a side effect of their design. Since online engagement is built on responses, the Viral Inquisitor demands that everyone relate to the truths of others.

People still select and deliver important content to one another, but content no longer takes the form of logical statements with truth-values that can be tested against the absolute truth. Instead, content becomes a vehicle for the expression of emotional attitudes. The automatic means of reaction, such as likes and reposts, on social media do not require logical deliberation. Under such a design, the point is to express the right attitude, not to convey true information.

---

[1] Logan, Robert K. (1986). The Alphabet Effect: The Impact of the Phonetic Alphabet on the Development of Western Civilization. See also: Alphabet effect. *Wikipedia*.

Wrong information is tolerated when it allows the right attitude. And the right information is ignored if it supports the wrong attitude. Confirmation bias is embedded in the design: we trust what we "like." This is why fake news victoriously marches across the Internet. The "truth" that has already been verified by viral distribution is too good to be fact-checked. The problem with fake news is not that it's hard to refute – rebutting it is often easy. The problem is that people like fake news. They vote for it with their clicks and their likes.

Under such truth-verification conditions, the truth of any story remains a matter of probabilities, but judgments are certain and real; they are "proved" by dissemination, and they are voted for and verified, in lieu of the story itself. Conspiracies thrive when truth gives way to attitudes and groupthink. Conspiracies gain as much power as is lost by objective truth.

Social media have completed the epistemological mutation of truth into post-truth. One can mourn absolute truth and the culture based on it, but society must learn to adapt to the conditions of crowd-sourced, negotiated truth. Digital truth's persuasiveness is more important than its rationale.

The Viral Inquisitor possesses algorithms that detect and report our preferences. It forces us into compliance and enables the next stage of digital development – the society of social scoring. The algorithms are good (and getting better) at detecting and tabulating our attitudes. For now, they decide what content to show us in accordance with our attitudes. Soon, they may use knowledge of our attitudes to tell us what to do. The viral inquisition will evolve accordingly. For now, the Viral Inquisitor still acts through the executive power of corporations and communities. Soon, the algorithms may merge with government power. Social scoring would then become the Viral Inquisitor's tool of discipline and punishment.

Social media emancipated authors, but to what end?

Platform capitalism is the hunt for "lazy authors"[1]

More than 4.85 billion people have access to the Internet. Online, they can find all the information available to humankind and form their own opinion regarding anything. The Internet has stripped authorities of any control over information they once had. This alone has radically changed society. But what disturbs the established order most is the new technological ability of the same 4.85 billion people to express themselves. It is not free access to information but free access to self-expression that changes the world. We are living through an unprecedented explosion of authorship.

We can gauge the scale of this explosion by estimating the number of people who were able to communicate their opinion beyond their immediate surroundings before the Internet. For example, the Google Books project[2] was aimed at digitizing all the books ever written. There was some debate about what counts as a book, but in 2010 the project came to the conclusion that humankind has written 129,864,880 books. According to other data, scientists have published about 50 million articles in academic journals since the end of the 17th century.[3] We can add about one million journalists and also all the politicians, marketers, academics and others who have conveyed their information beyond their physical reach. We will find that the estimated number of authors in human history before the Internet hardly exceeds 300 million (Figure 1).

---

[1] The essay is based on the article with the same title in Discourse. (2022, January 13). Revised for book publication.

[2] Taycher, Leonid. (2010, August 5). Books of the world, stand up and be counted! All 129,864,880 of you. Google Book Search Blog.

[3] Jinha, Arif E. (2010). Article 50 million: An estimate of the number of scholarly articles in existence. *Learned Publishing*. 23 (3): 258–263.

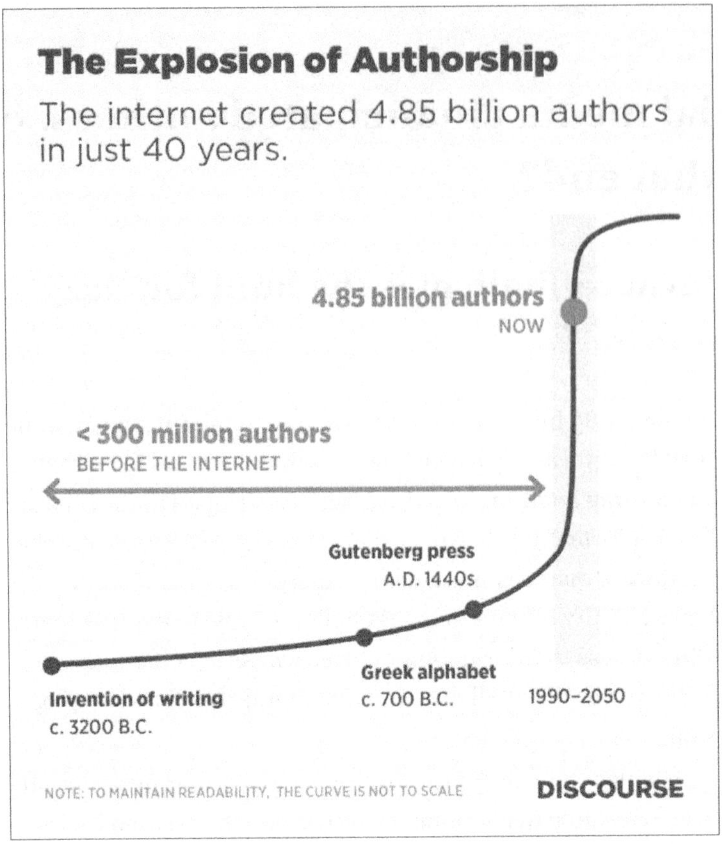

Figure 1. The explosion of authorship. Image credit: Discourse.

The chart above, derived from my book "Human as Media,"[1] gives us a picture of this explosion of authorship. Humankind had 300 million authors in 5,000 years of written civilization and, all of a sudden, this number has skyrocketed to 4.85 billion current authors in the span of just 40 years. Such authorship has given us unprecedented opportunities for self-expression, but it has also intensified that self-expression in ways that discourage thoughtful, measured responses and encourage polarization.

Authors at the gates

Besides their colossal numbers, these emancipated authors are characterized by a wide range of intentions and quality of output. At their

[1] Human as Media. The Emancipation of Authorship. (2014).

core, all 4.85 billion are authors only in the technical sense. They have acquired just the technical ability to contribute to content production and selection, even if only by clicking the "like" button. By itself, Internet access confers neither passion nor talent nor charisma. The noble authors of the past needed to have some outstanding quality to surmount the technical and social barriers of publishing. For modern authors, the Internet offers an opportunity to contribute at will.

Social media are specifically good at exploiting our Hegelian "struggle for recognition." As herd animals, we humans need to feel a sense of being together; hence our thirst for response. Social media provide, or at least offer, a response to even the most minuscule activity of a user. Their settings predefine our actions. The very environment of social media is designed to extract our activity in the form of likes, posts, reposts, comments – to extract any meaningful click from our online presence. That is why a contribution – even the contribution of a mere click – is not just an opportunity on the Internet. It is a duty, a condition of socialization in the modern world. I click, therefore I am.

Types of Internet authors

Social media create this environment to perpetuate our engagement so that, after getting online, we cannot reject being contributors. It's no longer a wonder or privilege – it's a daily routine. But the forms and degrees of this contribution vary widely. Several categories of emancipated authors are outlined below.

Flickering authors. These authors use the Internet mostly for browsing or personal communication. Flickering authors are on the periphery of emancipated authorship. Sometimes, however, they can kick into higher gear and like, share or even comment on someone's post, most likely that of a close friend.

Silent authors. These are the authors whose authorial activities do not involve typing. They contribute their unspoken opinions by pressing the "like," "share" and "repost" buttons. Along with flickering authors, silent authors, because of their vast numbers, have a significant role in content selection and distribution on the web.

Interjectional authors. The authorship of these contributors has a minimal material embodiment – it is mostly reduced to leaving an emotional mark of their presence, in the fashion of animals marking territory. This mark is most often an interjection: "OMG," "LOL," "WOW" or their surrogates, such as smiles, emojis, memes and GIFs. It is hard to gather much of a response from such a contribution, but the thirst for response is irrational; it runs behavioral activity anyway, especially when additionally encouraged by the design of a platform. A "wow" or a GIF can be likable – they can earn a "like," the token of digital reward for online activity.

Commenting authors. These contributors are enthusiastic enough to express themselves by producing more or less heavy content. But they are followers: They add something to something already said. This authorial activity needs a starting impulse from someone else. Commenting authors, however, represent the editorial and fact-checking potency of the Viral Editor – the dispersed, collective mechanism of content production, selection and distribution.

Emitting authors. These contributors have sufficient expertise, evidence, passion, and most importantly charisma, to start a discussion. Emitting authors sense trends and turn them into threads.

Principal authors. These contributors initiate not just discussions but discourses. They find the most resonating fibers in the social tissue and pull them out into the spotlight. Their most important characteristic is not just charisma but also autonomy: they need no one to launch discussions they deem important. They are the nonelected tribunes, though not necessarily on political issues.

These categories describe not so much types of personalities but rather types of media activities. A single user can act at different levels of authorial intensity. For example, a regularly silent author can suddenly jump to a higher level if he or she accidentally says something interesting to many. The very design of the social media platform encourages authors to perform a quantum jump into a state of higher media activity and become a commenting author or even an emitting author. But most people generally are comfortable within certain types of media activities. The descriptions of their authorial activity tend to become their personal characteristics.

One can suggest different classifications of author activity. What is important is that the media activity of 4.85 billion Internet users comes down to different intensities of employing their now-technologically-

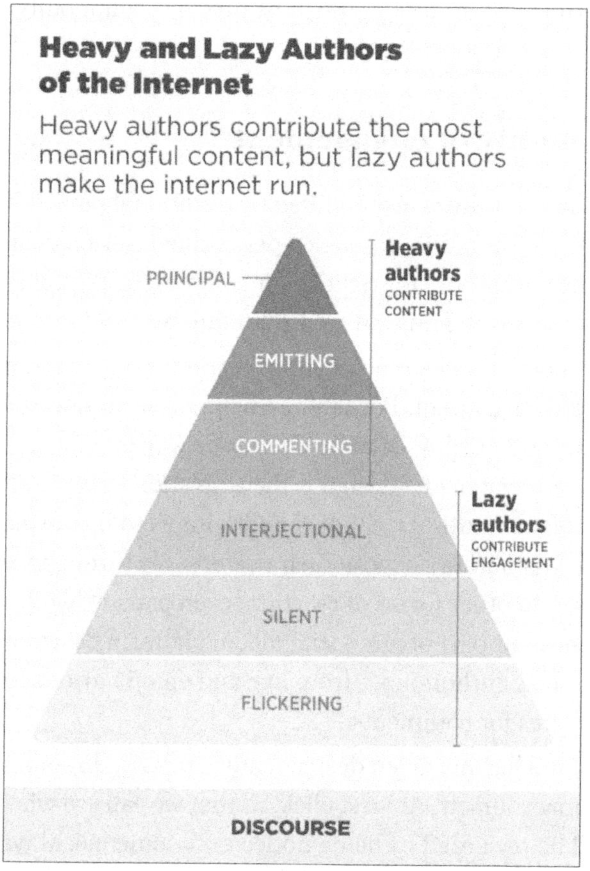

Figure 2. The pyramid of the heavy and lazy authorship of the Internet. Image credit: Discourse.

emancipated authorship. Ultimately, the categories boil down to heavy authors, who create the forms for their content, and lazy authors, who contribute their attitudes in the "pre-cooked" forms of engagement.

To put it simply, heavy authors contribute their content, while lazy authors contribute only their presence. But their presence differs from that of the silent audiences of the past, such as readers of physical books and magazines. Unlike those audiences, today's emancipated authors, even the laziest ones, can engage with the content in a variety of ways, ranging from a mere click or "like" to posting something of their own. Their engagement is what sustains social media and the Internet in general. Engagement materializes time and attention, the most precious commodity in digital capitalism.

The commodity of engagement

The Gutenberg culture, exemplified by traditional publishing, was based on heavy authorship. Its gatekeepers valued, selected, and encouraged heavy authors for political or commercial purposes. Digital capitalism, by contrast, aims at lazy authorship first and foremost.

Yes, designers of social media platforms offer incentives for heavy authors to produce content. For their activity, these authors gain recognition and opportunities to profit (in one way or another). But the "final cause" of social media design is the activation of lazy authors. Even the content of heavy authors, enabled and reinforced by the platforms, aims to make lazy authors expose their preferences through views, reads, likes, reposts, and other forms of reaction, even pausing while scrolling. The most important part of any social media platform design is to provide the means for lazy authorship – from like and emoji buttons to quizzes and colored templates for comments.

On social media, any given design feature insists: do something, react somehow, show yourself! At least click, so that we can see what you are. The click will be rewarded by being noticed. By someone. Maybe. And, for sure, any click will be registered, packed and sold in volume by algorithms. The instant reward of assumed recognition for the minuscule effort of a click is the fundamental mechanism of social network platforms, which improves the socialization of users and increases ad sales for the platforms' overlords.

The evolution of digital media does not reject heavy content. If someone is up to creating it, why not? After all, heavy content supplies engagement, too. But the efforts of digital media engineers are focused on activating lazy authors. They are the central figures of digital media.

The new media environment provides the greatest service of self-expression and self-actualization, the highest values in Maslow's hierarchy of needs. This gift of personal super-connectedness is hard to overestimate, especially amid the pandemic and recurrent lockdowns.

But with this great service comes great disservice. Social media seduce people into self-displaying at a statistically and historically unprecedented level, and we are left to deal with the consequences. Aimed to extract our engagement, social media intensify the self-expressions of millions. Those self-expressions are artificially exposed at a scale unseen before, and they spiral into additional rounds of reactions and self-expressions. Unprepared and unhesitant judgments regarding someone's personal matters or public affairs increase incredibly. Personal becomes public and public becomes personal. The excess of noise mutes moderate opinions and amplifies extreme views.

The very design of social media communication makes its content more likely to hurt than please its participants. Rage and polarization are inevitable outcomes in an environment where even the contribution of a click is reinforced – all for the sake of better ad customization.

Postjournalism and polarization

How the media polarized us. The shift from plentiful ad revenue to the desperate pursuit of digital subscriptions has turned journalism into postjournalism.[1]

Public trust in the media has hit an all-time low.[2] Common explanations for this crisis of credibility include bias, polarization, and fake news, but these causes are themselves effects of the tectonic, and generally overlooked, shift in the media's business model.

Throughout the twentieth century, journalism relied for its funding predominantly on advertising. In the early 2010s, as ad money fled to Internet platforms, publications sought to earn revenue through subscriptions instead of advertising. In the process, they became dependent on digital audiences – especially their most vocal representatives. The shift from advertising to digital subscriptions invalidated old standards of journalism and led to the emergence of postjournalism.

The golden age of the news media

Everything we once knew about journalism depended on the model of the ad-funded news media. Advertising accounted for most of the news industry's revenue during the twentieth century.

This business model provided a selective advantage to certain kinds of media. Since the revenue from copy sales was not sufficient to maintain news production, news outlets needed to attract advertising. As a result,

[1] The essay is based on the article "How the media polarized us" in *City Journal*. (2022, Summer). Revised for book publication.

[2] Salmon, Felix. (2021, January 21). "Media trust hits new low." *Axios*.

the media that relied mostly on the reader's penny, such as the working-class press, which was quite influential in the late 19th to early 20th century, were marginalized and eventually driven out of the market. The mass media that were oriented around the "buying audience" – the affluent middle class – received money from growing advertising and thrived.

In political economy, this selective effect is called "allocative control." The ad money did not tell the media what to do; it just chose the media that encouraged its audience to buy goods. Along the way, advertising money created the mechanism of discourse formation that Herman and Chomsky called the Propaganda Model (1988).[1] Seeking more advertising, the media maintained a context favorable for consumerism and political stability. Using Walter Lippmann's term, Herman and Chomsky claimed that the media "manufactured consent."

This business model was extremely successful. By the end of the twentieth century, the news media had reached the apex of their 500-year history. Even regional newspapers such as the *Baltimore Sun* possessed several well-staffed foreign bureaus. Never were the media as rich and influential as in their golden age, just 25 years ago. Plenty of journalists still on the job remember those glorious days.

Under the ad-based model, media capital represented a significant social force. It protected its interests, its market value, and therefore its independence. The abundance of money enabled newsrooms to develop an autonomy secured by the division between news production and ad-sales departments – a "glass wall" between ads and news. Preselected by ad money, news organizations geared toward affluent audiences became influential to the point that their independence determined their market value.

Ad money carried the risks of advertisers' pressure in news production, which would have undermined newsroom autonomy, a source of reputation and therefore capitalization. So, professional standards were elaborated to protect journalism from advertisers and establish the credibility of news coverage. Credibility was seen as a professional virtue but also as a commodity. "The theory underlying the modern news industry has been the belief that credibility builds a broad and loyal audience, and

---

[1] Herman, Edward S., and Chomsky, Noam. (1988). *Manufacturing Consent: The Political Economy of the Mass Media*.

that economic success follows in turn," declared the American Press Association in its 1997 "Principles of Journalism" statement.

Thus, paradoxically, the allocative control of ad money determined not only the allegiance of mainstream media to corporate elites (hence, "corporate media") but also sustained high-quality journalism. Newsroom autonomy was protected by the standards of objectivity, nonpartisan and unbiased reporting, attention to the arguments of all parties involved, investigative rigor, the separation of fact from opinion, and other guarantees enshrined in the ethical and professional codes of news organizations.

The same set of professional standards that was meant to secure credibility and independence from ad money turned journalism into a public service. "The central purpose of journalism is to provide citizens with accurate and reliable information they need to function in a free society," claimed the American Press Association's statement. "Commitment to citizens also means journalism should present a representative picture of all constituent groups in society. Ignoring certain citizens has the effect of disenfranchising them."

The only entity to which journalism was called to be biased against, even meticulously so, was power. This was a part of the credibility code, too. Endowed with these principles, initially rooted in ad funding, journalism evolved in the twentieth century as the "watchdog of democracy," positioning itself above partisan party struggle.

Another effect of advertising predefined the attitude towards the audience. If the audience was supposed to be affluent, mature, and able, so too were journalists expected to avoid judgment and patronising when reporting. The naked but thoroughly investigated facts and the positions of both sides were supposed to be presented to the public to judge. Hypocrisy and a sort of professional arrogance, of course, had always had a place in the profession. Journalists are generally prone to see themselves as priests and shepherds. Nevertheless, leaving the privilege of judgement to the readers was deemed to be one of the fundamental virtues of journalism at a time when it was funded predominantly by advertisers.

Advertising as a leading source of revenue predefined also the social-demographic targeting in the media. For better advertising reach, news coverage was supposed to broaden audience, not narrow it. The audience was regarded through the prisms of consumer profiling and cooptation, not political affiliation and separation. Potentially divisive political issues were downplayed.

All of this cooled the political activity of the public. Observing the state of the media in the 1990s, Robert McChesney called his book *Rich Media, Poor Democracy*, describing the low degree of participation in elections as "democracy without citizens." If the medium is the message, then the message of the ad-funded news media was "buy!" – not "vote!" or "protest!"

The political passivity of the masses might have seemed to be bad for democracy, but polarization in society was at a low point, while the influence and prosperity of the media were at an all-time high. Capitalism generously paid the media for promoting consumerism and manufacturing consent. Political tranquility was a side effect – detrimental or benevolent, depending on one's perspective

The collapse of advertising

The Internet broke this idyll. It turned out that the ad-based model relied not on the content attracting an affluent audience but on the monopoly over ad delivery that the Internet simply destroyed. It took a hundred years for the ad-based media business to achieve power and prosperity; it collapsed in just ten.

The collapse started with the classifieds. At their peak in 2000, classified ads brought in $19.6 billion,[1] about one-third of newspapers' revenue.[2] Craigslist, eBay and others killed this market by offering people a better service for free. Classifieds revenue plummeted to $2.2 billion in 2018.[3] Thus, $17 billion was wiped out from newspapers just because consumers had migrated to better platforms with the same (actually, better) functions.

Corporate advertising was the next to go. Suddenly, firms found that they could reach their desired audience directly and precisely, with full control over content, context, and targeting.

---

[1] Reinan, John. (2014, March 3). "How Craigslist killed the newspapers' golden goose." *Minnesota Post*.

[2] Pew Research Center. (2021, June 29). Newspapers Fact Sheet.

[3] U.S. Census Bureau, Breakdown of Revenue by Advertising Type: Newspapers Advertising Space - Classified Advertising for Newspaper Publishers. *FRED, Federal Reserve Bank of St. Louis*.

Finally, Google and Facebook delivered the fatal blow. Old media used to offer advertisers a costly and inefficient carpet-bombing advertising. Unlike the news media, Google and Facebook know the personal preferences of each user and provide the personally customized delivery of ads to billions. In 2013, Google alone made $51 billion in ad revenue. That year, American newspapers' ad revenue was $23 billion, and the global newspaper industry collected $89 billion in ad revenue. The Google-Facebook duopoly surpassed 60 percent of the share in the U.S. digital ad market in 2018.[1] It became increasingly clear that old media had no chance of competing with digital platforms. Digital platforms offered a completely different scale, cost, accuracy, and efficiency of advertising.

Ad revenue in the US press hit rock bottom in 2013. It plummeted below the level of 1950, when the industry started measuring the print ad market. [2] The addition of digital ads was insignificant and did not save the day.

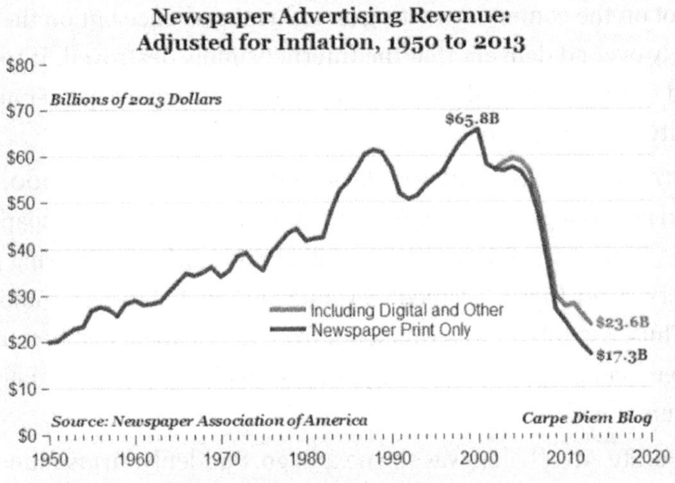

Figure 3. Calculations by Mark Perry,
The American Enterprise Institute.

---

[1] Dang, Sheila. (2019, June 5). "9 months ago Google, Facebook have tight grip on growing U.S. online ad market: report." Reuters.

[2] Weissmann, Jordan. (2014, April 28). "The decline of newspapers hits a stunning milestone." Slate.

In 2016, the Newspaper Association of America stopped reporting newspapers' annual ad revenue: this source of revenue had basically ceased to exist. Residual advertising in print media, both offline and online, lost its industrial scale. Today, advertising contracts in some news media often resemble charity from ideologically aligned businesses.

Not only did ad revenue collapse to historically low levels, but it also plummeted below the level of reader revenue. This happened simultaneously around the world. In 2014, ad revenue in the global newspaper industry ($86.5 billion) trailed reader revenue ($92.4 billion) for the first time in the history of industrial measurement. Even the strongest American newspapers could not hold advertisers: the *New York Times* began getting more revenue from readers than from ads in 2012.

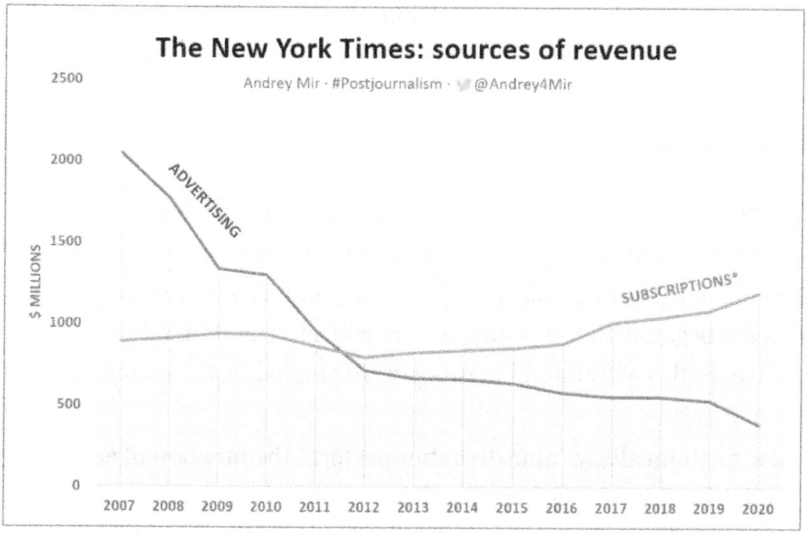

Figure 4. Ad and reader revenues in the New York Times. Source of data: The New York Times Company.[1]

Observing the catastrophic occurrences in the industry, Robert McChesney wrote in the foreword to the 2015 reissue of his 1999 *Rich Media, Poor Democracy*: "The marriage of capitalism and journalism is over." The era of classical journalism was indeed over. The media were no

[1] The New York Times Company's press releases.

longer “rich”. But did democracy stop being “poor”? Divorced by capitalism, who did journalism start seeking in marriage instead?

Some publications invested their hopes in ancillary businesses – from organizing conferences to selling wine – but these markets were already saturated. Literally everyone else, each business, sells “something else” and, thanks to the Internet, themselves become media.[1] Some publications courted philanthropic billionaires or public funding, but the handful of high-profile survival stories could not arrest the dynamic of decline.

After desperate and entertaining attempts to secure atypical funding, the news media returned to their natural and only remaining source of revenue: selling content. But the issue was that selling print subscriptions and copies at stands was no longer a viable option. News consumption had already moved to the Internet and social media. Losing ad business and having no support from print subscriptions, news orgs turned to their last hope – digital subscriptions. They started wooing the digital audience.

...Digital who?

But who was the digital audience at the time, in the early 2010s?

Social media had already spread around the world. The demographic of social media in their initial phase was very specific. The proliferation of social media began with the young, urban, educated, and therefore progressive. Both Twitter and Facebook were created by the young, for the young.

A new medium always aims to better perform the function of an old medium. In the case of social media, they were meant to enhance chatting, dating and socializing. But then a new medium also always starts imposing its own unforeseen features. Thus, the second major effect of social media came to life: a part of users’ socialization evolved into activism and politicization.

Social media accelerate socialization by enabling an instant response from others to any user’s activity. Seeking a response, users strive to find, produce, and share interesting facts, evidence, opinions, and expertise – whatever can trigger the response of others. This creates a dispersed

[1] Mir, Andrey. (2014, November 16). Content marketing: How companies are turning into media. Case study. *Human as media Blog*.

mechanism of mutual informing that I call the Viral Editor.[1] This mechanism indeed does the job of the editor, as it selects, refines, and delivers socially relevant content by collective efforts in the process of viral distribution (hence "viral").

The Viral Editor of social media created an alternative environment of news supply. Led by the pioneers of digital activism, the urban educated progressive youth started shaping an alternative agenda for themself. Before long, they revealed how significantly their agenda differed from the agenda of the old establishment in the mainstream media. These two types of agenda-setting always contradict each other. Sooner or later, the contradiction grows into the question of agenda control. And this is a political question. Politicization on social media was inevitable. [2] It happened always and everywhere simply due to the morphological differences in agenda-setting between legacy media and social media.

This morphological discrepancy in agenda-setting can be metaphorically described as a clash between the Pyramid and the Cloud.[3] The Pyramid represents the established institutions of authority that are financially maintained by corporations and ideologically maintained by the mainstream media. The Cloud, in turn, represents the multidirectional, versatile, oscillating forces born in the live interactions of peers and is structured and embodied by the Viral Editor.

The power of the Pyramid is based on top-down hierarchical distributions of material resources. The power of the Cloud is based on the coagulating contributions of information resources. These are incompatible forms of social organization. When the Cloud gains sufficient potential for self-recognition, meaning its own agenda, it simply cannot tolerate the Pyramid.

The greater the differences between the agendas shaped by social media and by the mainstream media, the more intense the clash between the Cloud and the Pyramid becomes. Between 2009 and 2014, the alternative agendas induced on social media became so powerful that they

---

[1] Mir, Andrey. (2013, November 13). The manifesto of the Viral Editor. Human as media blog.

[2] I explored the inevitable development of social media use from socialization to activism and politicisation in Human as media. The emancipation of authorship. (2014).

[3] Mir, Andrey. (2019, December 25). The Pyramid against the Cloud: Institutions' perplexity regarding the Net. Human as media Blog.

produced a "crisis of authority," in the words of Martin Gurri, who described this as the "revolt of the public."[1] The Viral Editor agitated the digitized, urban, educated, and progressive youth to the point of political indignation. Protests, and even revolutions, broke out across the globe, including the Arab Spring (2009–11), Occupy Wall Street (2011), the "social justice" protests in Israel (2011), the Indignados protest in Spain (2011), the student protests in Greece (2010–11), the anti-Putin protests in Moscow (2011–12), the Taksim Square Protest in Turkey (2013), and many others.

Each of these events had its own set of causes, of course, but all had several features in common. First was the specific demographics of the protesters – the digitized urban educated progressive youth. Second, the protests generally opposed the establishment, regardless of ideology, from Hosni Mubarak's and Vladimir Putin's regimes to the U.S. economic and political system during Barack Obama's presidency. Social media elevated the role of progressive discourse producers, including all kinds of artists, trendsetters, young academics, and activists. The main social feature of the new medium – the intensity of self-expression in the pursuit of response – tended to saturate private talks with public concerns and thus empowered activism as a mind-set, not just an activity.

The very design of social media has made activism highly socially contagious. Yes, people contaminated each other with certain ideas. But most importantly, they infected each other with a mode of action – with the necessity of self-expression, which was environmentally driven to judge public matters and escalate toward extremes due to the increasing noise and decreasing receptiveness. This was the true message of this new medium. In the 2010s, activism gained momentum in digital media and proliferated far beyond its traditional circles.

Seeking to please the digital audience

Such were the conditions in which legacy media began looking for business opportunities in a new digital environment. To sell digital subscriptions, they needed to find ways to attract ***this*** digital audience (as there was simply no other digital audience at the time).

---

[1] Gurri, Martin. (2018 [2014]). *The Revolt of the Public and the crisis of Authority in the New Millennium*.

This is not to say that journalists were complete strangers to the digital public. On the contrary: journalists usually come from the ranks of urban, educated, and progressive elites. Many of them were themselves social-media pioneers. Journalists, therefore, were naturally predisposed to align with the dominant ethos of early social media – in part, because they "have always been more liberal than their fellow countrymen," as Batya Ungar-Sargon pointed out in her 2021 book *Bad News*. "But in the past," she maintained, "this liberalism was checked by their publishers, who were often the owners of large corporations, or Republicans, or both. They wanted their newspapers and their news stations to appeal to the vast American middle, which meant that journalists were not at liberty to indulge their own political preferences in their reporting." [1]

Indeed, the ad-based business model had kept the natural liberal predisposition of journalists in check. The balance between the liberalism of the newsrooms and the business necessity to appeal to the "vast middle" for better advertising maintained both the market value and cultural power of journalism. Despite the inherent liberalism of many journalists, the need to address the largest affluent group of consumers – the middle class – led journalism to elaborate on and strictly follow the professional standards of objectivity and unbiased investigative rigor. The highest examples of that work – such as the Watergate investigation, the Pentagon Papers, and the Boston Globe's "Spotlight" investigation of sexual abuse in the Catholic Church – bolstered the professional reputation of the news media.

Yet the essential ingredient of that recipe – the advertising-dictated necessity to appeal to the median American – had disappeared by the early 2010s. The inherent liberal predisposition of newsrooms was suddenly unchecked by any financial imperative. Now the news media needed to appeal to the digital progressives. Furthermore, social media provided an unprecedentedly efficient tool for news gathering. This was an extra stimulus for journalists' immersion into social media discourses dominated by the progressives at the time.

In his famous 2011 theses, "Ten tweets to transform newspapers," publisher John Paton (who issued the call "Digital First!" for the industry) stated: "...Trust the crowd & especially your youngest employees: they will

---

[1] Ungar-Sargon, Batya. (2021). *Bad News: How Woke Media Is Undermining Democracy*. Encounter Books. P. 7.

lead the needed experiments."[1] And so the media naturally did: they submitted to the digital crowd and younger demographics; the digital crowd happened to be the younger demographic, eager for societal changes.

Ten Tweets to Transform Newspapers

John Paton, at MediaXchange 2011, March 26

1. The newspaper model is broken & can't be fixed.
2. Newspapers will disappear in less than10 years unless their biz model is changed now.
3. The new newspaper model must become digital first and print last.
4. The new newspaper model must now only allocate resources to the new news ecology.
5. Stop listening to print people and put the digital people in charge – of everything.
6. Newspapers must invest in content, sales & disruption – sell or outsource everything else.
7. Trust the crowd & especially your youngest employees they will lead the needed experiments.
8. Complaint: newspaper dollars becoming digital dimes. Response: start stacking the dimes.
9. Digital First works: #jrc digital audience grew 75% now more digital audience than print in less than 1 year.
10. Digital First works: #jrc digital revenue up 70% Q1 '11 vs Q1 '10 – real growth not newspaper voodoo bundling metrics.

Figure 5. "Ten Tweets to Transform Newspapers" – Digital First! manifesto by John Paton, 2011. Digital First! seemed to bring incredible growth in the beginning, as this was growth from a very low base. Bottom line: Digital First! affected policies but did not save the business.

The cultural proximity between journalists and the progressive users of early social networks, the news-gathering power of social media, and the need for media organizations to secure digital subscriptions led to an ideological convergence between the majority of large media organizations and digital progressives. As a result, the principles of news coverage changed dramatically. Coverage became determined not by the necessity to reach out to the "vast middle" but by focusing on pressing social issues highlighted by the progressive Twitterati. Quantitative studies cited by Ungar-Sargon indicate that the use of terminology associated with woke politics, such as "racism," "people of color," "slavery," "white supremacy," and "oppression," has skyrocketed in the American mainstream media precisely since the early 2010s.[2] This radical shift affected the entire news

---

[1] Paton, John. 2011, March 26. Ten tweets to transform newspapers. IndieWire.

[2] Ibid. P. 4.

ecosystem. TV and radio needed to "go digital", too. They started developing their own digital addictions and dependence on digital crowds.

Frequency of words denoting prejudice in the press

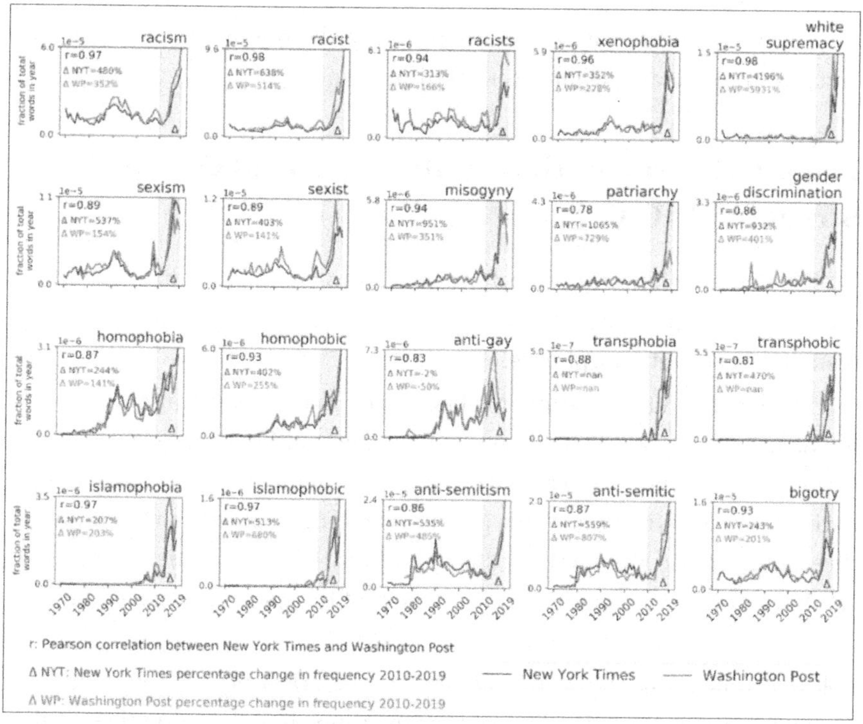

Figure 6. The frequency of prejudice-denoting terms in the New York Times and the Washington Post news and opinion articles, by Rozado et al.[1] *In total, the study analyzed word use in 27 million news and opinion articles written between 1970 and 2019 and published in 47 of the most popular news media outlets in the United States and detected similar patterns. The study registered the statistical change in language and the synchronization between the media but did not make any connection to the political economy of the media. The surge, however, clearly correlated with the Digital Rush – the switch of the news media from plentiful ad revenue to desperately seeking digital subscriptions in the early 2010s, when the digital audience had very specific social-demographic characteristics: mostly white, urban, educated, and progressive youths.*

---

[1] Rozado, David, Al-Gharbi, Musa, and Halberstadt, Jamin. (2023). Prevalence of prejudice-denoting words in news media discourse: A chronological analysis. Social Science Computer Review, Vol. 41(1), pp. 99–122.

This happened historically instantly between 2010 and 2016. In terms of social effect, the loss of advertising and focus on the digital audience resulted in a shift of the media from representing a broader populace to representing its digitized and most progressive part.

This ideological transformation, however, did not bring the media any much-awaited financial gains until Trump came.

The Twitter revolution continued: from Occupy Wall Street to MAGA

Thus, the metamorphoses of the media did not happen during Trump's presidency. On the contrary, Trump's ascension was, in no small part, the result of these metamorphoses.

The key to understanding this lies, again, in the demographics of social media use. Comparative data on social-media proliferation suggest a hypothesis that the online activity of a certain demographic group can lead to the political activation of this group if the group exceeds an "awareness threshold," to use Martin Gurri's terminology.[1] This "awareness threshold" can be defined, very roughly, as when 60% of the group uses social media.

In the demographics of "urban", "age 18–49" and "college educated", this "awareness threshold" was passed around 2009-2011. They were digitally "activated" and politicized. At the time, digital progressives still identified with a new, decentralized political subculture that opposed the establishment. Soon enough, however, the attention of the mainstream media propelled the digital progressives into a discourse-formation role not just for the urban, educated digital youth but for the entire society. The marriage with the mainstream media granted the digital progressives an entry ticket to the establishment. In a matter of several years, digital progressivism resettled from the Cloud to the Pyramid, from a posture of rebellion against centralized power structures to one of alliance with them.

Meanwhile, social media continued to grow and proliferate. By 2016, the next demographic wave of social media users – older, less urban, less educated, and therefore more conservative – reached the "awareness threshold," with 60% of the group using social media.

---

[1] Gurri, Martin, (2018 [2014]). *The Revolt of The Public and the Crisis of Authority in the New Millennium.* P. 53.

Now the digital conservatives became a part of the Cloud – the new Cloud. In the same vein as their younger predecessors 5-6 years before, the digital conservatives acquired access to agenda-setting. Soon enough, they discovered that the agenda, imposed by the newly formed alliance of the mainstream media with the digital progressives, completely ignored their views and values. The news media embraced an unheard-of stance: they marginalized the majority.

Similar to their younger predecessors, the digital conservatives "evolved" from idle talks to political outcries. Excluded from the mainstream agenda, they grew resentful. Their indignation coagulated into a socially significant force seeking release. It is the same mechanism that underlay the Arab Spring and all early Twitter revolutions. In terms of media ecology, Trump's ascension completed the Occupy Wall Street movement, but on a different demographic base.

The rest is well known. Donald Trump, with his TV instincts for popularity and having no political agenda whatsoever, sensed the demand. He quickly tweaked popularity into populism, gained incredible media attention for free, made himself a channel for conservative indignation, and enabled the release of the already built-up resentment pressure of the conservative Cloud, disregarded by the mainstream media due to their romance with the digital progressives.

Mutation into postjournalism completed

From 2010–2011, when the leading media began introducing paywalls, until 2016, digital subscriptions remained insignificant from a business perspective, especially amid the hopes that were placed in it. However much the news media wooed the digital progressives, it was not until the conservative demographics arrived on social media that the news media started scoring in digital subscriptions.

The reason was that the ideological alliance of the media with the digital progressives could not bring commercial returns. The digital progressives were indeed progressive – they did not consume news from old media. News and ads were delivered to digital audiences through other platforms. The mainstream media had no commodity to offer their newly chosen reference group, nor could they profit from selling this audience to advertisers.

Trump helped fix the lack of business relations. He became that missing commodity immediately after his shocking victory in November 2016. The mainstream media recognized the signal, upgraded Trump from amusement to existential threat, and started selling the Trump scare.

Importantly, the relationships were not transactional. The news media did not ***sell*** news about Trump – this news was always already known to any digital user from social media news feed. Even though the news media supplied the news there, users received it for free, leaving little opportunity for the traditional business model of selling news. Instead of no longer viable transactional news sale, the news media quickly learned to solicit subscriptions as support for a noble cause – the protection of democracy from "dying in darkness," as the Washington Post put it.

A new business model emerged – soliciting subscription as donation to a cause.[1] Donations required triggers, so the media supplied those triggers. The crucial part of the new business model was not just Trump himself but the significant number of his supporters. The most terrifying thing was that fully half of the electorate supported such a "monster" (in the view of the other half). The news media joined the political battle.

The media were by no means interested in mitigating this divide. On the contrary, they needed to maintain frustration and instigate polarization to keep reader-donors scared, outraged, and engaged. Basically, the news media turned to confirming how outrageous the outrageous news were. Their focus shifted toward such news almost entirely. Checking the disturbing value of disturbing news meant that the mainstream media switched from ***news supply*** to ***news validation***. This was a clear sign of the mutation of journalism. It started turning into postjournalism.

It all was about Trump, of course, but both ends of the political spectrum were involved. Right-wing outlets also tried to sell scare instead of news – the scare of losing ground and country. The new business model made the media the agents of polarization. They organically joined to the mechanisms of polarization that had formed in the larger media environment – on the Internet and social media.

The validation of disturbing news within certain value systems had finally become a viable business model. Some mainstream media grew

---

[1] I examine this business model in *Postjournalism and the Death of Newspapers. The Media after Trump: Manufacturing Anger and Polarization*. (2020).

their digital subscriptions severalfold during Trump's tenure. This surge in subscriptions was labeled the Trump Bump.

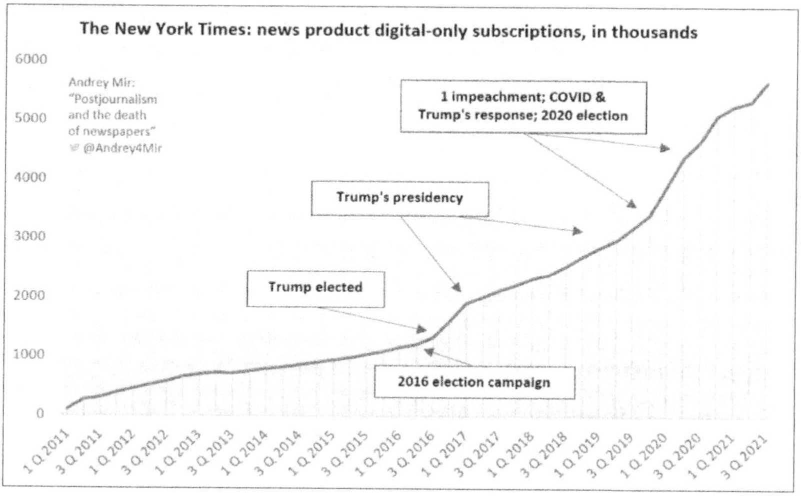

Figure 7. The New York Times: news product digital-only subscriptions (in thousands). Source: The New York Times Company's press releases[1].

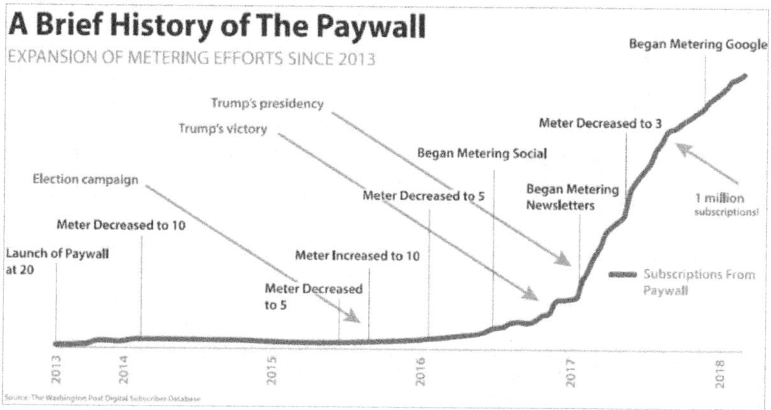

Figure 8. Correlations between the growth of the Washington Post's digital subscriptions and marketing strategy – or Trump-related events. Source: World News Publishing Focus, WAN-IFRA[2]; Trump-related events are added.

[1] The New York Times Company's press releases.

[2] Veseling, Brian. (2018, July 30). Washington Post puts emphasis on creating paths to subscription. *World News Publishing Focus, WAN-IFRA*.

However, this business model brought significant results only to the largest media outlets. The reason is that news validation creates a swarming effect. People want to have disturbing news validated by the most authoritative news notary, whose validation expertise is accepted by as many people as possible. For the validation of news about Trump, audiences were willing to pay only to flagship media outlets like the *New York Times* or the *Washington Post*.

All other, smaller media outlets had to join the chorus, not because of the carrot of digital subscriptions, but rather due to the stick of digital backlash if they did not. Most subscription-donation money flows to a few behemoths. Soliciting subscriptions as donations to a cause led not only to media polarization but also to media concentration. Data show that only the largest mainstream media outlets could benefit from this model. All the rest continued to decline even amid this Trump Bump.

Newspaper	2002 print circ	2019 digital subs
The New York Times	1,113,000	2.7 million
Los Angeles Times	965,633	170,000
The Washington Post	746,724	1.7 million
New York Daily News	715,070	27,000
Chicago Tribune	613,429	100,000
Newsday	578,809	25,000
Houston Chronicle	552,052	37,000
The Dallas Morning News	521,956	72,000
San Francisco Chronicle	512,129	57,000

Figure 9. Only the largest news outlets succeeded in digital subscriptions. Source: Joshua Benton, NiemanLab[1]; Benton made a reservation saying he was as generous as possible in interpreting some numbers, as they may include double-counted subscribers.

[1] Benton, Joshua. (2019, July 31). "The L.A. Times' disappointing digital numbers show the game's not just about drawing in subscribers – it's about keeping them." NiemanLab.

There is always a temptation to blame the increasing media biases on some "coastal elites", corporations, Murdoch, alt-right conspiracy, or whoever else fits the role of a boogeyman. All those actors were involved, but the real driving forces lie much deeper. The Internet has destroyed the old business model of the news media, which was based on advertising. The Internet has also deprived the media of the opportunity to sell news. The media began chasing the digital audience and fell into an ideological trap that altered the standards of news coverage, leading journalism to mutate into postjournalism – soliciting support for a cause under the guise of informing. The death of newspapers that shut down before this mutation was at least honorable.

Journalism wanted its picture to fit the world. Postjournalism wants the world to fit its picture. This is essentially a definition of propaganda. Postjournalism has turned the media into crowdfunded corporate ministries of truth that joined the political struggle out of desperate business need for survival. If the ad-driven media manufactured consent, the reader-driven media manufacture anger. The former served consumerism; the latter serve polarization.

It is common to conclude an analysis with a solution. There is no "solution" for a media shift of such magnitude. "How do we fix polarization?" is the wrong question. The right question is, "How are we going to live with it?"

The evils of empathy

Social media compel empathic involvement, and the overproduction of empathy increases tribalism and decreases tolerance.[1]

Legend has it that in the early years of Facebook, Mark Zuckerberg told the news feed developers: “A squirrel dying in front of your house may be more relevant to your interests right now than people dying in Africa.”[2] It sounds terrible, but what he likely meant was that, in this new medium – the Facebook news feed – personal news should acquire the significance of traditional news and take its place.

At the time, in the late 2000s, it was a revolutionary move with a clear purpose to reverse the traditional understanding of news. Focusing on close-range personal events instead of some terrible but distant suffering was received as a lack of empathy, allegedly promoted by the tycoons of new media. But Zuckerberg’s alleged comment was really about technical settings: the news feed was supposed to prioritize personal over public content, to the degree of disregarding even significant information if it did not involve the user’s social graph (“friends”).

Focusing on personal matters at the cost of public concerns clearly set the social media news feeds apart from traditional media. This, not the lack of empathy, was the intention. In fact, however, social media have drastically increased the level of empathy in society – to the extent that empathy has begun to erode social relations.

Empathy as a media effect

Knowingly or not, Zuckerberg echoed a similar metaphor used by Adam Smith 250 years earlier. In his 1759 treatise “The Theory of Moral

---

[1] The essay is based on the article with the same title in *Discourse*. (2024, May 24). Revised for book publication.

[2] Stone, Zara. (2016, October 10). 11 times Mark Zuckerberg kept it real. *Forbes*.

Sentiments," Smith suggested that the prospect of losing one's own little finger would disturb a man much more than the death of "a hundred millions of his brethren" swallowed by a sudden earthquake in China. Though this sounds callous, it makes sense: of course, personal, immediate experiences or even the anticipation of such experiences evoke much stronger emotions than distant events, no matter how dramatic. (Smith utilized this emotional distinction between personal and distant events to construct his theory on how morality almost "rationally" emerges from personal interests through sympathy and compassion.)

Comparing a distant disaster with a personal feeling, Smith could not have taken into account the emotional power of media portraying distant news. He simply didn't have language for it. How would people in the 18th century learn about a disaster in China? In Smith's words, "Let us consider how a man of humanity in Europe, who had no sort of connection with that part of the world, would be affected upon receiving intelligence of this dreadful calamity." Obviously, the "intelligence" would have been delivered via rumors, personal correspondence or, at best, early newspapers.

Naturally, the strength of sympathetic feelings comes either from the immediacy of the drama or from the means of its mediation – in other words, from media. The emotional impact of news differs when conveyed through oral speech, reading, photos, or television. The emotionality of the news is the product not so much of the news content, but rather of the medium through which this news is conveyed. In mediated communication, empathy is a media effect. By their very design, media determine the level of empathy in society; they also determine the distance empathy can reach. Additionally, by selectively transmitting content, media also define who gets our empathy, increasingly in terms of "worthy" and "unworthy" victims, to use the terms Herman and Chomsky coined in their Propaganda Model to describe the empathic discernment of the media.

For example, a textual medium favors conveying information, not emotion. Lacking the ability to represent content vividly, as oral narration or pictures would do, text requires the linear and sequential organization of content. The need to sift the content through the organizing efforts of the writer imparts a certain degree of rationality to the content. This is why text always favors rationality over emotionality, as compared with oral speech, for example. To make a text emotionally impactful, additional poetic efforts are required. Books, magazines and newspapers need to use pictures and graphic highlights to amplify the emotional impact of printed text. News about a horrifying yet distant disaster, delivered via text, would affect readers, of course – especially when distant news is scarce in general – but the rational and detached mediation of text always diminishes the potential for emotional perception from reading.

Media-induced empathy ended industrial wars and rekindled tribalism

Media theorist Marshall McLuhan used the term "empathic involvement" to describe the psychological effect of retribalization in the global village[1] – the world united and agitated by electronic media. Unlike reading, television engages viewers emotionally rather than rationally. TV immerses viewers in a situation through watching and listening, thus recreating the environmental immersion typical of orality (in contrast to the environmental detachment typical of literacy).

It was not a coincidence, for instance, that the Vietnam War ended after the proliferation of television. Vivid images of atrocities fueled the anti-war movement. This did not happen with the somewhat similar war in Korea a decade earlier – TV hadn't been there yet. Television, with its empathic power ended the era of the imperialist wars, the bloodiest ones in history. There have been no full-scale industrial wars after Vietnam. Instead, the era of "hybrid wars" began. The level of empathy maintained in society by the medium capable of broadcasting "live" pictures has rendered unacceptable the industrial butchering of armies and civilians. Full-scale war is no longer politically or morally accepted. Because of media, wars now try to disguise themselves as various forms of anti-terrorist or military "operations."

Television immerses people in a mode of perception where they have to sympathize, admire, be angered, be frustrated, and experience the entire spectrum of emotions. The same was the mode of perception in tribal orality. In tribal settings, however, empathic involvement served as a mechanism of survival. People had to be emotionally tuned-in for better collective interactions. Rapport was the foundation of cohesion and tribal unity. Today there is no survival need for people to physically synchronize

[1] McLuhan, Marshall. (1962). *The Guttenberg Galaxy*. P. 39.

immediate collective perception while watching TV. Television restored the empathic involvement of orality, but only technically, due to its capacity for emotional immersion.

But this technicality had brought enormous social and cultural impact. Being just a media effect, empathic involvement has nevertheless reintroduced tribalism, to which it was a "natural" cognitive and social regulator. Empathic involvement has synchronized the emotions and attention of the audience and made these personal traits available for commodification. TV incites empathic involvement not only to capture viewers' time and attention, but also to build their loyalty and even addiction, the most valuable assets in post-industrial capitalism. The loyalty of the masses to certain media consumption easily converts into various business models. You can sell something to a loyal audience or sell a loyal audience to advertisers or politicians. Television made possible "affective economy,"[1] in which Marx's classical formula evolved into its post-industrial form: "money – affect – money."

As soon as the media effect of empathic involvement was commodified, it turned into a self-sustaining loop of positive feedback. The more empathic involvement was commercialized, the more it was produced. The commodification of empathic involvement caused "behavior modification" – the term that computer scientist Jaron Lanier suggested to substitute for "advertising."[2] Society was increasingly trained to be compassionate – by the medium, for profit.

That's why Zuckerberg's statement suggesting that a nearby event should receive higher priority in the news feed than a distant tragedy was poorly received by the public. Its "technicality" was missed, but its alleged callousness was read. However, the technical intent behind this statement seemed to fail, too. Yes, social media started conditioning people to see publicly exposed personal news as more relevant in the news feed than public news. But the result turned out to be unintended: instead of focusing on the personal, the news feed ended up personalizing ***any*** shared news, including public news. By technically prioritizing personal relevance over public concerns, this new medium made public concerns overly personal.

---

[1] Ahmed, Sara. (2004). Affective Economies. Social Text, Duke University Press, 79 (Volume 22, Number 2), Summer, pp. 117-139.

[2] Lanier, Jaron. (2018). *Ten Arguments for Deleting Your Social Media Accounts Right Now*. P. 31.

The overproduction of empathy

The effect was tectonic: digital media made society even more empathetic than electronic media did. People learned to experience distant news not through detached text, as in the Gutenberg era, but in their personal agenda within their most intimate space of communication – the screens of their personal devices. Zuckerberg is lucky that this statement was attributed to him in the late 2000s, not now, in the mid-2020s. With today's level of mandatory empathy in society, any prominent person would be destroyed for comparing the death of a squirrel with deaths in Africa.

Whereas television emotionally immersed people in news through watching and listening, social media added talking. The "emancipation of authorship"[1] by the Internet made people themselves into media. Now the social media users not only consume empathic involvement – they produce it.

The affective economy of television was based on the formula "money – affect – money"; social media have upgraded the formula to "money – engagement – money." Television offered everyone empathic involvement in the shared public agenda; social media have made users demand empathic engagement from one another. Any activity on social media is a request for affirmation, submitted to others.

Seeing social media as a devilish device is common but wrong. Social media provide users a unique and precious service of accelerated self-actualization through the responses of others – the highest value in Maslow's hierarchy of needs. The theory of Dunbar's number posits that the primate brain can maintain meaningful connections with 120-150 individuals, roughly the size of a small tribe or village – or the number of acquaintances an individual could make in a lifetime. Social media overrode Dunbar's number. Facebook, for instance, allows 5,000 friends and thousands of followers. Never before has humankind been able to create or maintain such an ample amount of friendship.

But this explosion of socialization comes with a price. The cognitive capacities designed for 150 meaningful connections are overwhelmed. The social equilibrium based on slow, lifelong socialization is destroyed. On

---

[1] Mir, Andrey. (2014). *Human as media. The emancipation of authorship*.

social media, empathic engagement is no longer an affordance – it's a duty. As users are immersed in an environment where they not only demand responses from others but also are demanded to respond to others, "agonistic mentality"[1] becomes the basic emotional tone of interactions. The explosion of socialization has become the implosion of passive (or not so passive) aggression: the empathic demands from around the world have surged into the user's perception, customized and amplified by algorithms and the user's own network of friends.

The commodification of affect (by television) and engagement (by digital media) created empathy without unity. It retrieved the emotional involvement that was typical in an oral – tribal – society, but on the technological basis of a new medium that provides distant empathic involvement without any real personal connection and without any physical limitations of space and time. Social media tribes are virtual – most members have never met one another, never really liked one another, and never needed to like one another for any practical purposes of interaction. Their fictional need for tribal coherence is induced by the medium that extracts their tribal identities for commodification and makes people think that their identities matter more than their deeds, that their identities are their deeds (for social media ad targeting, they are). Empathy without unity amplifies animosity. People attack one another with their requests for affirmation, causing an empathy race in which empathy gets inevitably weaponized.

As Lanier suggested in his 2018 book *Ten Arguments for Deleting Your Social Media Accounts Right Now*, "Social media is destroying your capacity for empathy."[2] It is indeed so, but not because social media lack empathy. Quite the opposite – social media compel users to empathic involvement. The resulting oversupply of empathy simply devalues it, leading to empathy-policing by everyone toward one another, ensuing mass anger and polarization.

Sociologist and philosopher Jean Baudrillard noticed a similar phenomenon in 1981: "We live in a world where there is more and more

---

[1] "Agonistic mentality" is a term used by Walter Ong to describe a feature of the oral mind. See: Ong, Walter. (2002 [1982]). *Orality and Literacy*. P. 43.

[2] Lanier, Jaron. (2018). *Ten Arguments for Deleting Your Social Media Accounts Right Now*. P. 73.

information, and less and less meaning."[1] The same dynamic is now seen on social media: we live in a world where there is more and more empathic involvement, and less and less real empathy.

If you can't return to text, be a cat

If the amount of empathy is predefined by the dominant medium, then what medium would slow down the overproduction of empathy in society? Text, of course. Reading isolates vision from the other senses and turns the sensory faculty of vision into the cognitive capacity of inner vision. Walter Ong, a scholar of literacy, called it the "inward turn." Historically, the inward turn of literacy enabled individualism and thus destroyed the primeval tribal immersion of people. With the proliferation of writing, prehistoric tribal society came to an end.

Unlike the oral mind, the literate mind focuses on meaning and not on empathic synchronization with others. Written text is subject-matter-oriented, not relation-oriented. Empathy is not inherent in writing in the way that it is innate in both primary and digital orality. Society could have alleviated the overload of empathic involvement if it had returned to more reading, as it did in the Gutenberg era, called the Age of Reason not without reason.

But a return to text is impossible. Deep and long reading will never regain its position of dominance now that humans have tasted digital devices. Digital media are much more efficient than writing or print in communication, socialization, and accumulation of knowledge. Most importantly, they are much more hormonally rewarding, as every click is supported by a dopamine micro-hit. No reading can compare with the annoying yet addictive pleasure of digital surfing, scrolling, and clicking. Humankind will not be able to repeat that transition from relation-oriented orality to content-oriented literacy that happened in the Axial Age 2,500 years ago, when literacy started replacing primary orality.[2] The media era of rationality has gone irrevocably.

---

[1] Baudrillard, Jean. (1994 [1981]) "The implosion of meaning in the media," in *Simulacra and Simulation*, translated by Glaser, S.F. Ann Arbor: University of Michigan Press. P. 79.

[2] I examine this shift from orality to literacy and its today's digital reversal in *Digital Future in the Rearview Mirror: Jaspers' Axial Age and Logan's Alphabet Effect*. (2020).

Speculating about the loss of meaning due to oversupply of information in the 1980s, Baudrillard concluded that the system could only reproduce itself and escalate: "There is no alternative to this, no logical resolution. Only a logical exacerbation and a catastrophic resolution."

Contemplating the reasons for deleting one's social media accounts, Lanier suggests a solution based on a metaphor of dogs' and cats' characters. Dogs are emotionally very responsive and amenable. They have no options other than dissolving into the collective behavior of a pack, most likely highly agitated. Be a cat, suggests Lanier. It means less empathic involvement. Being a cat is a substitute for reading when reading is gone.

A modest proposal for Elon Musk

Set a 280-character minimum for tweets[1]

The public is guessing what Elon Musk will do with Twitter when he acquires control, assuming his $44 billion acquisition of the social media platform is finalized. One thing seems clear: the standard profit motive is scarcely relevant. Private acquisition tends to involve extra motives, especially for socially significant businesses such as the news media or social media. Musk seems to be buying Twitter in no small part to set the rules – and specifically to reset the standards of free speech.

The question troubling some of the public seems to be whether Musk will restore former president Donald Trump's account. That is a trap that will be hard to avoid. But beyond the issue of Trump, Musk's assumed motives behind buying Twitter seem obvious. As ex-Reddit's CEO Yishan Wong recently speculated,[2] Musk may indeed long for the days of the early Internet.

Figure 10. A tweet by Yishan Wong, ex-Reddit's CEO. April 15, 2022.

---

[1] The essay is based on the article with the same title in *City Journal* (2022, April 26).

[2] A tweet by Yishan Wong. (2022, April 15).

Twenty years ago, Internet mavens wanted merely to change the old world. The blogosphere was a frontier where people could freely express themselves, and censorship by large corporations controlling the means of discussion was unheard of. Today, social media have become a cultural battleground where speech is circumscribed, often by authorities – especially speech that these authorities reject – but also by many users, who seek to silence or suppress speech of those they deem unworthy of it.

It seems, indeed, that Elon Musk is determined to do something about that. What exactly? He is already exciting to promise some new features regarding bots or algorithms. [1] But will they really address the core issues of Twitter and social media in general? The only way to fix Twitter may be to turn its basic design upside-down.

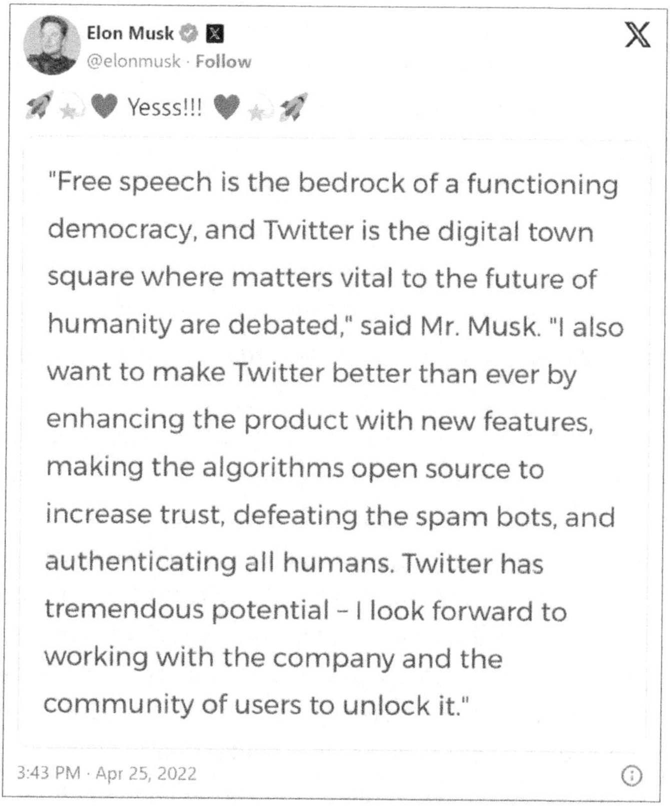

Figure 11. A tweet by Elon Musk, April 25, 2022.

[1] A tweet by Elon Musk. (2022, April 25).

The Internet emancipated authorship: it gave everyone an opportunity to communicate their views far beyond physical reach. Moreover, what had appeared to be a technical opportunity for reacting and self-expression turned into a pressing necessity. Social networks' business model depends on users' engagement. Every feature – be it a "like," a "repost" button, or a news feed algorithm – aims to boost this engagement.

Since users' physical time is limited, more engagement means shorter interactions and faster exchanges. On social media, quick replies with shorter messages inevitably result in an outpouring of emotion. Conversations increasingly involve not a sequence of well-thought-out sentences but emotional signalling full of exclamations, interjections, and their digital substitutes (emojis, memes, gifs, and videos). Post-literacy has collapsed into digital orality. The exchange of exclamations is hardly suited for thoughtful expression, but it is a good vessel for emotional rampages. The form invites a certain type of content. Thoughts have been replaced with attitudes that, to be noticed through the noise, tend to gravitate towards the extremes.

Rage and polarization, then, are embedded in the very business model of social media. They are not flaws of human nature or politics; they are a media effect propelled by the technological affordance of the medium and the business necessity to maintain this medium and profit from it.

Two strategies can reduce polarization: ***media literacy*** and ***media engineering***.

Media literacy helps people understand that rage and animosity are more the product of media, not people. These are not people from the left or the right that would like to annihilate each other. This is a systemic platform design that causes people to lean to the extremes for better engagement. "Users" aren't equal "humans"; human nature is more complex than that. Social media turn, for profit, regular people into users with exaggerated attitudes and amplified identities. Awareness about the distinction between media's effects and human nature, ideally, would encourage people to moderate themselves and tolerate others.

But media literacy could slow down the engagement of how many? Tens of thousands? Hundreds of thousands? It might help them but will not eliminate the technical cause of rage and polarization. There are almost

5 billion users on social media. A solution is needed that will impact the behavior of billions. If someone manages to slow down the exchange for, let's say, two billion – the total population of Facebook, Instagram, and Twitter – polarization would subside in a month. A solution of this scale is possible only at the level of media engineering. Whoever finds such a solution will deserve the Nobel Peace Prize because it would reverse the very logic of media evolution.

What would such a solution entail? At the core of any participatory digital medium lies a fundamental factor that makes instant participation possible: the speed of message delivery. Reversing this trend is the key to making media saner.

Electric communication cancelled space and released time, formerly needed for a message to travel. "Information moved at electric speeds also sends the sender instantly," wrote Marshall McLuhan. "Not just the broadcaster but his public go to Peking and return, and everybody becomes totally involved in everybody."[1] Electric media give humans the god-like conditions of a "disembodied spirit," or "the angelic discarnate man of the electric age who is always in the presence of all the other men in the world." Reactions to any occurrences are no longer limited by either physical or social distance. With instant access to everyone and each other, everything becomes debatable.

McLuhan foresaw the consequences. According to him, electric speed has turned the world into a global village "where everybody is maliciously engaged and poking his nose in everybody else's business."[2] On another occasion, McLuhan wrote,

> The global village absolutely insures maximal disagreement on all points... The spaces and times are pulled out from between people. A world in which people encounter each other in depth all the time. The tribal-global village is far more divisive – full of fighting – than any nationalism ever was.[3]

---

[1] Marshall McLuhan in a letter to Father Shook, as quoted in: Chrystall, Andrew. (2011). After the Global Village. *The Canadian Journal of Media Studies*, 9 (1).

[2] An excerpt from the movie: *This Is Marshall McLuhan: The Medium Is the Massage*. (1967). Directed by Guy Fraumeni and Ernest Pintoff. 17:00.

[3] McLuhan, Marshall. (1997 [1967]). The Hot and Cool Interview to Gerald Stearn. In Michel A. Moos (Ed.), *Media Research: Technology, Art, Communication: Essays / Marshall McLuhan*. p. 57-58.

Media engineering to reduce polarization need not mean the filtering of participation or content, for then the possibility of censorship emerges. Engineers should instead target the speed of engagement. If instant engagement inevitably favors emotionality, disagreement, rage, and polarization, then the inhibition of engagement affords space for deliberation, rationality, tolerance, and collaboration.

History suggests as much. Culture itself is the inhibition of natural reflexes. Delayed reactions allow observation, consideration, and planning. Imagine two people playing chess via snail mail. Normally, chess is a race against time, but when players cannot respond immediately and must think about their next move, they are encouraged to spend more time contemplating it. The inhibition of response leaves – indeed, creates – room for deliberation.

Generally, all communication media before electricity developed to speed up communication through space but kept reactions delayed in time. Writing and print favored deliberation because they allowed huge distances to be covered at the cost of slowing down message production (as compared with spontaneous speech exchange). As media ecologist Paul Levinson put it in his book *Human Replay*,[1] "Until the telegraph, not a single technological medium permitted such an immediate interchange of information." Even letter exchange, a form of writing directly based on interactivity, made "each party respond to the other in segregated absentia." The first electric communication medium, the telegraph, allowed "anyone to hook into the system to immediately interact with anyone else hooked into the system." As Levinson concludes, "The telegraph thus broke once and for all the observational yoke that had been the unavoidable burden of all previous technological extensions [of humans] across time and space."

With electric and now digital media, the response time in communication has caught up with the reaction time of natural reflexes or spontaneous speech (hence "digital orality"). The individual's nervous system has extended to the size of the planet, as McLuhan predicted. Through digital media, we can instantly react to events with no space constraints or time delays.

But this comes with a price. We are returning to our primitive mode of instantaneous communication, in which complex semantics of verbal

[1] Levinson, Paul. (2017). *Human Replay: A Theory of the Evolution of Media*. P. 188.

expression had not yet emerged, and signaling dominated. Except now, the tribe is global. Instead of sharing observations, users share their exaggerated identities in the growing noise of everyone's omnipresence. The design of social media extracts our basest attitudes, not our thoughts, in order to sell us to advertisers and politicians.

Is it possible to reverse this process? Technological solutions do exist. In 2020, Twitter tested prompts that encouraged users to pause and reconsider a potentially harmful or offensive reply before they hit "send." When given such a prompt, 34 percent revised their initial reply or decided not to send their reply at all. Twitter also began prompting users to read an article before retweeting the link to it.[1] But these all were drops in the bucket. For a radical change in settings affecting billions of interactions, a solution is needed that will strike at the core – at the essential features of the platform design.

So here is the promised piece of advice to Elon Musk: set up a character ***minimum*** for tweets. The fundamental feature of Twitter is its limit of 280 characters for a post. Brevity was considered a virtue for a writer in the print era, but on Twitter, brevity has nothing to do with a sender's virtue. Quite the opposite: short tweets tend to be short on rationality. In this medium, brevity is a business gimmick that makes the news feed faster and easier to engage with. What is needed to reverse radically this feature of social media is an opposite limit: tweets must not be ***shorter*** than 280 characters. A quantum of media[2] must once again become time-consuming, inhibiting responses via technical delay, into which thoughts, not only emotions, might be squeezed. (Alternatively, Twitter could prioritize longer posts.)

This would encourage an unthinkable outcome for social media: requiring a user to think about what to write. And that renders it extraordinarily unlikely. After initial hype, such rules would undermine engagement, which lies at the core of Twitter's business model. It can also accelerate the growing dominance of non-textual media alternative, such as TikTok.

---

[1] Butler, Anita, and Parrella, Alberto. (2021, May 5). Tweeting with consideration. *Twitter Blog*.

[2] See Chapter "The quantum theory of media" in *Postjournalism and the Death of Newspapers. The Media after Trump: Manufacturing Anger and Polarization*. (2020).

Therefore, solutions that slow down social media engagement cannot be driven by market imperatives. A source for such solutions, though, might be the arbitrary will of an eccentric owner – one who does not care much about the platform as a business and whose ambitions are peculiar enough to include sending humans to Mars.

The dark side of the screen

Our computers' journey away from dark to light screens – and back again – shows how digital media influence human behavior.[1]

The recent Super Bowl marked the 40th anniversary of the groundbreaking Apple Macintosh 1984 commercial that changed not only advertising but the way we use digital devices. Among other things, Apple introduced the light screen to simulate habitual print pages and seduce us into digital usage. Since then, many people have defaulted to using the light mode on their device screens. Some of them didn't even know that there was an option to set up a dark background. To them, the dark mode was an aberration. Why would somebody use the dark mode, so unnatural for reading?

Figure 12. Image credit: Discourse.

Now, however, more and more users are switching to the dark screen. Why are people offered this choice? How do they choose the dark mode or

[1] The essay is based on the article with the same title in Discourse. (2024, February 14). Revised for book publication.

the light mode? These questions of digital anthropology can shed light on the tectonic transition from the print era to the digital world.

Nocturnal creatures

One hypothesis is that the divide between light-screeners and dark-screeners is mostly generational. Older people are digital migrants: we came from the Gutenberg era. The rationale of keeping the light mode on for screens is obvious – this format simulates the appearance of a book page. Many digital migrants would not have even imagined that it could be otherwise. In the print era, a black background with white letters served only as an artistic technique predominantly employed in posters. It's close to impossible to read a significant amount of text in such a manner.

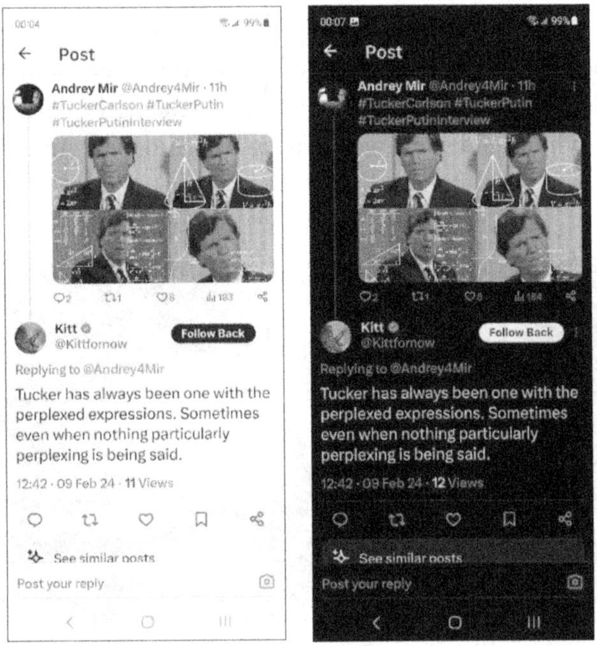

Figure 13. This is how the same tweet looks in dark and light modes.

Digital natives, in their turn, will likely lean toward a dark screen. There are two primary reasons for this. First, the era of print dominance ended before their time, so black inks on a white page do not hold sway over them. Second, and more importantly, a black screen is genuinely more convenient at night, and night use was the original purpose of the dark screen option. Another name for dark mode is "night mode." It was assumed that users would switch between the modes according to the lighting conditions.

But I bet nearly nobody does it. The alleged convenience of adapting the screen to different lighting conditions is fairly insignificant compared to the annoyance of changing settings twice a day. So, those who choose the dark mode, whether due to the absence of a book-reading habit or due to their technical proficiency and open-mindedness, will likely stay with this mode around the clock.

The apparent generational divide, however, does not encompass all the nuances behind choosing to use a dark vs. a light screen. The most surprising aspect is that, technologically, if true to its nature, the screen ***should be*** dark, not bright. The very emergence of the light screen mode was a global conspiracy of media aimed to seduce humans into the use of this new medium.

The light in the darkness

A sign may be defined as a meaningful mark on a meaningless background, a deliberate effort amid inherent nothingness. In terms of energy expenditure, the symbol is "1" while the backdrop behind it is "0." That is why the screens of computers and other electronic devices were initially dark. If a sign is an active effort on a passive background, then electric marks must be made by firing pixels, gas microtubes, glower filaments or whatever can be illuminated by an electric impulse. Just as it was "natural" for written and printed media to have dark ink on a light page, it is "natural" for an electric screen to be dark with glowing symbols on it.

Indeed, the first computers mostly had dark screens. They followed the logic of energy efficiency, not consumer accommodation. Here lies another cultural divide behind the light and dark screen users. Programmers, the creators of the digital world, are more likely to opt for a black background. Ordinary consumers, who use computers for other needs, are more likely to use the light mode. By introducing the light mode, technologically unnatural to screens, computers have accommodated nonprofessional users from the mass market.

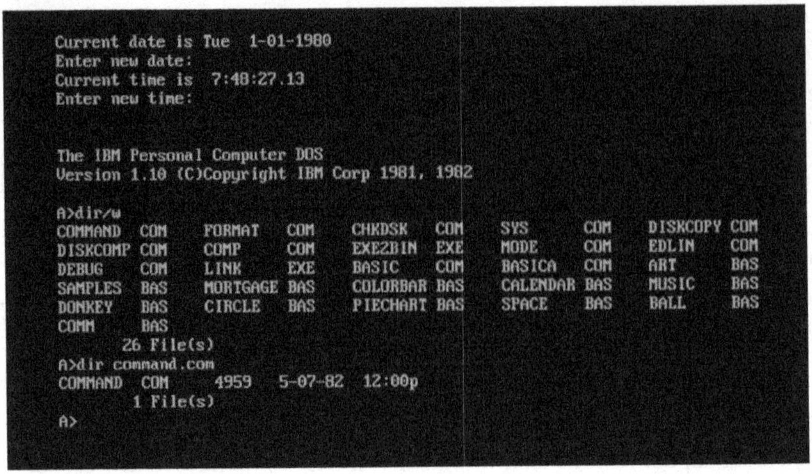

Figure 14. IBM PC DOS. Version 1.10 (1982) command line. Image credit: Wikimedia Commons.[1]

Let there be light

We can pinpoint exactly the moment in history when programmers ceased to dominate the population of computer users, and the number of ordinary consumers grew enough to become a new target for computer design, leading to the advent of light screens. This "demographic" shift occurred on January 24, 1984, when Steve Jobs introduced[2] the public to the Macintosh – the first computer specifically geared toward mass consumers and devoid of the burden of "programmer-centric" heritage in its design.

Apple Macintosh made "the computer for the rest of us."[3] It had a graphical interface (with pictures) and a mouse, allowing users to interact with any spot on the screen immediately, without running the cursor along the lines and characters. Accommodating regular users led to the emergence of a new principle of computer design: "what you see is what you get." The very idea of graphic design made the light background inevitable.

---

1 IBM PC DOS. Wikipedia.

2 Gallagher, William. (2023, January 24). Macintosh launched on Jan 24, 1984, and changed the world – eventually. Apple Insider.

3 Interface Experience: Apple Macintosh, 1984.

Figure 15. 1984 Super Bowl Apple Macintosh commercial by Ridley Scott.

Digital mythology attests that Apple's team, with Jobs himself, might have gleaned the idea while visiting Xerox.[1] Xerox had been primarily known for its copying technology, introduced for commercial use in the 1950s. However, concerned about competition from the Japanese and fearing that business would become paperless in the future, the company created a computer division, which in 1973 developed the world's first desktop computer with a graphical interface and a mouse.[2]

Perhaps Xerox's attachment to paper and office paperwork was an additional factor that prompted the white background of its first graphical interface. In one way or another, the likely involvement of a paper-centered digital corporation in the transition from naturally dark screen interfaces to the paper-like light screen can be considered a kind of Easter egg from the perspective of media evolution. Regardless, the Xerox computer was quite expensive and never took off. Perhaps people at Xerox did not have that Steve Jobs' instinct to think of the consumer, not just of the product and its functions.

[1] Christoph. (2010, March 22). Did Steve Jobs steal everything from Xerox PARC? *Mac History*.

[2] Interface Experience: Xerox Alto, 1973.

The resemblance of the screen to the printed page with pictures represented a crucial cultural change. The computer industry turned its face to consumers, not programmers. IBM also transitioned[1] from MS-DOS to Microsoft Windows, a consumer-centered interface. And something profound happened: digital media, born with a dark screen and illuminated symbols, learned to simulate paper to lure billions of people from the paper era into the digital world.

Figure 16. An IBM PC 5150, pre-light mode.
Image credit: Wikimedia Commons.[2]

There was no other rationale for the light mode. Computers did not need it. To communicate with programmers, a dark MS-DOS screen with illuminated symbols worked just fine. But a few thousand programmers using computers cannot ensure the development of the digital industry and, consequently, the ongoing progression of digital media. Media evolution needs billions of users who make entrepreneurs invest billions of dollars in the development of new media. This is why media evolution has made computer screens light.

However, a question arises. Yes, light screens seduced the print-trained humans and expanded the demographic of computer users from thousands of programmers to already almost 5 billion consumers. Why, then, is a dark

---

[1] Weiss, Juliette. (2017, April 4). A brief history of Microsoft design. Microsoft Design.

[2] File: IBM PC 5150.jpg. Wikipedia.

mode back now? Is it just a generational shift, with younger users having less attachment to books? Is it because they increasingly use social media at night, in the dark? These factors undoubtedly play a role. But there is something else lurking in the darkness of the screen.

Light-on vs. light-through

In the 1960s, Marshall McLuhan famously stated that "The medium is the message." It was (and still is) a hard statement to understand. While teaching media at Fordham University, McLuhan's son, Eric, faced the same issue: The students struggled to comprehend why the medium itself is the message. In 1968, Eric McLuhan and his colleagues conducted the so-called Fordham Experiment,[1] which demonstrated how different media can convey different messages from the same content. Specifically, the experiment was intended to explore the differences between the perception of TV and cinema.

Students were divided into two groups. In the same room, the same film was projected onto a semi-transparent screen. One group sat on the side illuminated by the projector's light, and the other sat on the opposite side – the image "shone" on them through the screen. So, the same movie was projected in "light-on" and "light-through" modes. The light-on mode recreated the typical conditions of "physical" perception – light fell on a surface and shaped images that were perceived by the eye. The light-through mode represented the principle of the electronic screen: light falls on the eye, passing through the screen with information.

The Fordham Experiment revealed significant differences in audiences' perception. The main distinction lay in the level of audience engagement. Those watching the movie screen (light-on) perceived what was happening on the screen as alienated events, as objects of observation. They felt more detached from the content and were able to judge the content more rationally and analytically.

Those watching the same film *through* the screen, with the light directed at them, were more immersed in what was happening on the screen. Reflecting on their viewer experience, they placed greater emphasis

[1] McLuhan, Eric. (2000). The Fordham experiment. Proceedings of the Media Ecology Association, 1, 23–27.

on the emotional aspects of perception. They also found it more challenging to correctly evaluate the duration of the film.

In one instance, when the students were watching Buster Keaton's comedy "The Railrodder" (1965), a participant from the TV group (light-through) even went to the other half of the room to see what the movie group (light-on) was laughing at. It was not that funny on his side, so he wanted to make sure that the other group was being shown the same film. Keaton, nicknamed "The Great Stone Face," was known for making comedy without a single smile. On the light-through side, involvement placed the viewers in the picture and diminished the comic effect, while the viewers on the light-on side remained detached observers and got all the fun intended by Keaton.

The Fordham Experiment showed that when the light shines on the screen or object, it allows the observer to stay more detached, whereas the light that carries information and shines on the viewer favors better immersion in that information. Visual detachment favors rational, abstract and analytic perception. Visual immersion favors immediate reactions that are likely more emotional and spontaneous.

Screen instead of sun

The very principle of light-on belongs to the physical world. Everything is lit up by the sun, and this is how we see things – their shapes reflect sunlight. In the digital world, however, information itself glows, lighted up by electric impulses.

As soon as digital media outgrew the programmer demographics, they began to simulate not electric but physical "illumination" of information to seduce billions of users into digital media consumption. Their "purpose" was to activate market forces for further development of digital media.

But the current comeback of the dark mode indicates that humankind is approaching the final stage of resettling onto the digital. Perceiving information that itself glows is becoming more common than perceiving information that is lit up. Digital media no longer need to simulate physical lighting conditions, so they are reverting to their natural format – the dark mode.

Two centuries ago, electricity began erasing the distinction between day and night, replacing humans' naturally lit environment with an artificially lit one that is totally controlled by human media activity rather than the "activity" of the sun. Now the information glowing from digital screens is completing this transition from the sun-dependent environment to the screen-dependent environment.

The dark screen, carrying information in light-through mode, no longer unaltered by the simulation of sunlight, not only accommodates media consumption that ignores the "natural" reality of day and night but also enables better and stronger immersion of the users in the reality of the screen. Information glowing onto us users diminishes our ability to perceive objects in a detached way and to control the time spent in media consumption. We invest more time and effort, fully immersing ourselves in digital media. While some decry our screen "addictions" and increased detachment from the physical world, this is precisely what digital media need from us to continue to evolve.

The medium is the menace

Ubiquitous digital media offer potent rewards – but at the price of eroding our sensory and social capacities needed in physical reality.[1]

Marshall McLuhan held that every medium constitutes an extension of our physical or mental faculties. The hammer extends our fist, the spear our teeth, the hut our skin, the wheel our feet – and electronic media our central nervous system. By broadening human intellectual and social faculties far beyond our natural abilities, the Internet has given us incredible benefits. Our abilities to search for information, memorize, socialize, and even make friends have been massively enhanced. Never before could humans augment their knowledge of any subject matter so quickly and easily. Never before have people had so many "friends."

But everything comes at a price. Extended abilities provide new power while disrupting the existing balance in our perception of reality. We humans can suddenly do more, reach further, and hence receive more signals from the environment than before. Neither the brain nor the sensorium is ready for it. This explains the psychological and social shocks that are always delivered by new media.

The increased sensory inputs cause an imbalance in the old sensorium and lead, in McLuhan's terms, to the "numbing" and "amputation" of organs and skills formerly responsible for certain tasks. A phone's digital memory remembers phone numbers for us, but it cuts off the part of our organic memory responsible for basic recall. Devices do many things much more efficiently than people once did, but they atrophy bodily functions, disrupting not only the preexisting sensorium but also old physical skills and social habits. Ubiquitous digital media, with their new reward system, threaten even more troubling changes. As the digital generation naturally replaces the predigital one, humankind is altering its neurophysiology, sensorium, and morality.

---

[1] The essay is based on the article with the same title in City Journal. (2022, Winter). Revised for book publication.

3,000 years of tech whining

Weighing the gains and losses that new media produce is an old tradition. In Plato's *Phaedrus*, god-inventor Theuth brought the gift of letters, which he created for people, to King Thamus for approval. Theuth claimed that writing would make the Egyptians wiser and improve their memory. Thamus replied that writing would actually cause forgetfulness because people would "not remember of themselves" – they would rely on the external written characters instead of their memories. Writing would become "an aid not to memory, but to reminiscence." People would learn a lot but know nothing. They would appear wise know-it-alls but lack real wisdom.

Both mythological figures proved right. Clearly, any recording devices cause personal memory to deteriorate, just as Thamus warned; however, collective memory has improved beyond measure, which seems to support Theuth's stance. Yes, people these days do not need to memorize phone numbers or birthdays – the smartphone will remind them. Is this good or bad? Personal faculties have deteriorated, but that's because media now perform their functions and are much better at it. The body's former capabilities are becoming media's functions.

The discussion of the merits and demerits of technology has continued ever since Plato. It has flared up recently, as the pace of technological change has accelerated. The speed has amplified the shock, making the arguments of the techno-skeptic Thamus more tangible. In the 1990s, the Internet was praised as a great repository of knowledge. In the 2000s, it was hailed as an environment of free communication. But since the 2010s, it has often been considered a danger – both to people and institutions.

The entire evolution of our species can be seen as nothing but an evolution of our media. As our powerful extensions, media deal with the environment much better than our naked selves. The logic of our faculties' migration into media, extended far enough, leads to a complete human resettling into media.

The migration of physical abilities to, say, a stone axe dealt with only a tiny fraction of our needs. Therefore, the "axe" had to evolve. And thus, we made every effort to develop our media. Unlike an axe or any implements of the past, the Internet caters to all human collective and personal activities. It is easy to resettle onto the Internet these days. We are nearly all the way there, except for some physical daily routines.

By increasingly taking over our body's work to accomplish more physical and intellectual tasks better and faster, media are freeing up our time, allowing us to spend that time on... consuming and developing media. It's a form of symbiosis. As McLuhan said, "Man becomes, as it were, the sex organs of the machine world, as the bee of the plant world."[1] In exchange for developing them, media offer us "nectar" in the form of conveniences of all sorts.

We're not just spending time on the Internet – we are investing time in its improvement. Every time we click a link, react to a story, or share it with others, we help the Internet evolve, like a bee pollinating flowers, in McLuhan's formulation. By improving the relevance of online content, our day-and-night labor of clicks enhances the Internet's convenience for us, which, in turn, strengthens its power over us.

The neurophysiology of digital enslavement

All this labor is changing us. Digital media alter not only our habits but also our brain's physiology. The human brain contains an estimated 100 billion neurons, each connected to others by hundreds of synapses. Brain activity consists of the electrochemical "firing" of neural circuits between neurons. Stronger or repeated experiences reinforce the burned-through links; neurons that fire together wire together, creating neural connections, the foundation of our brain's work.

Nicholas Carr, the author of the 2010 book titled *The Shallows: What the Internet Is Doing to Our Brains*, shows how the Internet is transforming our neurophysiology. Even seemingly similar activities, such as reading from a book or reading on the Internet, cause different neurological reactions. As research has shown, book-reading activates brain regions responsible for speech, memorizing, and processing visual information. Hypertext "reading" activates the brain regions responsible for problem-solving and decision-making.

As Carr notes, this might be beneficial for elderly people. Indeed, because of their lower mobility, older people live in a familiar, limited space, and they face few intellectual challenges and make few new

---

[1] McLuhan, Marshall. (1994 [1964]). *Understanding Media. The Extensions of Man.* The MIT Press. P. 46

acquaintances. For them, habits, the absence of novelty, and lifelong wisdom generally reduce the necessity to make decisions. Suddenly, the Internet has burst into their lives and forced their brains to do labor that is unusual for their age. Even the idlest web-surfing still requires making hundreds of micro-decisions. To click or not to click? That is now the question. To like or not to like? To comment or not to comment? This mental labor is similar to solving the simplest puzzles and lasts as long as a person is online. This keeps the brain alert and alive at the physiological level, forcing it to "fire up" new synapses. Micro-adjustments of the brain continue – a condition that was extremely unusual for the elderly in the offline world, where they had simply never experienced such a massive torrent of mental micro-tasks.

This neurological exercise is not prescribed by a doctor. This labor is not assigned by a boss. Merely being online makes users, including those long ago retired, work for digital capitalism – without any consent but also without any significant effort.

The decisions regarding clicks are tiny and require no physical strain. More importantly, they reward the brain with hormonal pleasures related to curiosity and socialization, which have always been an important part of the survival code of social animals. Curiosity leads us to find food and territory, while socialization ensures propagation and protection. The body has learned to encourage curiosity and socialization through the release of hormones that incite pleasure. That is why we feel elated when we make a discovery (as in Archimedes' "Eureka!") or receive recognition (hence the Hegelian "struggle for recognition").

Amazingly, digital media have "extended" these hormonal faculties. To get more of our time and engagement and to maintain its evolution, the Internet has appropriated our hormonal stimuli by offering so much material for curiosity and so many opportunities for socialization that we would never have found offline. By interacting with our hormonal system, the Internet offers us a flow of micro-stimuli in exchange for our engagement, which consists of micro-decisions about the relevancy of clicks, likes, reposts, etc. The pleasure received as a reward for curiosity and socialization is minuscule and hardly noticeable, but it is sufficient to keep us on the Net.

For older people, the benefits probably outweigh the harm. Their newly obtained devotion to the online environment is unlikely to cause serious damage to their offline abilities. For everyone else, though, the realignment of behavioral stimuli to digital stimulation with micro-rewards may endanger their offline well-being and even safety.

The issue with instant reward

When a user sees a reaction from others, thoughtfully facilitated by social media designers, the brain receives a hit of dopamine, a neurotransmitter that induces pleasure to reward certain behavior. According to a study[1] conducted at the UCLA brain-mapping center, an fMRI scanner showed "significantly greater activation in parts of the brain's reward circuitry" when teenagers see "likes" given to their pictures. A scan observed neuro-patterns similar to those seen when a person views pictures of loved ones or wins a small amount of money in the lottery. We want to experience new likes, resembling a gambler constantly pulling the handle of a slot machine in the hope of the next reward. And the "slot machine" keeps rewarding. Little by little.

Instant gratification for online activity drives the user engagement required for Internet platforms to be profitable. But when practiced almost eight hours per day (the time spent by an average American online), this behavior also forms a habit – a neuro-disposition, adjusted to certain interactions with the world. The brain rewires itself, enjoying instant reward for little effort.

In the physical world, rewards were naturally delayed and demanded greater effort – conditions to which the brain was accustomed. The delayed gratification for efforts in the physical world was typically well-deserved and provided stronger, more distinct pleasure. The hormonal rewards from food, sex, curiosity, comfort, socialization, and creativity brought vivid excitements. The link between effort and reward was often multilayered, too. For example, sex required the hard labor of building relationships, but with that could come love and the comfort of family life. Reading a book by Dostoyevsky took serious mental effort but delivered the joy of intellectual epiphany and the benefits of social status.

Unlike rewards in the physical world, the reward of a click is as trifling as the effort expended. The low quality incites a huge demand for quantity: sensing a hint of pleasure but never satiation, people spend more and more

[1] East, Susie. (2016, August 1). Teens: This is how social media affects your brain. CNN.

time online. This is a feature, not a bug: the new medium benefits from our increased engagement with it. Each action of a user, even their inaction, such as pausing scrolling, improves the customization of the Internet for this user. The growing engagement of bees-users increases the Internet's relevancy, enabling it to provide us with even more convenience and enhancing its ability to enslave us so that we keep developing the Internet and its devices even further.

The meagreness of the click's reward and the need to get further drawn into the process of click mining for more reward exhausts the body both physically and emotionally. More importantly, when people adjust to existing in the digital world, they lose the skills needed for living in the "slow" physical world and in a "slow" offline society that rewards only significant efforts associated with endurance, diligence, and resilience.

The loss of reading, shrinking attention span, and weakened concentration are only superficial manifestations of the brain's adaptation to the click's instant reward. The socio-forming effect of instant rewards for little effort lies in replacing the factor of effort, which regulates the physical world, with the factor of presence, which regulates the online world.

The moral principles of the physical world imply a reward for what one does. The moral principles of the digital world imply a reward for what one is – basically, for identifying themselves to others and algorithms. The identified presence (which often requires just a click) is already sufficient "effort" to maintain engagement, the Internet's main asset. This is why digital society is refocusing to reward the "effort of presence." Digital platforms need it as plants need the mere presence of bees. It is not a coincidence that, in digital capitalism, users' clicking is their labor. The click transforms user existence into user presence and produces engagement that, in the material form of data, gets expropriated and commodified by the platforms.

Thanks to digital media, the difference between effort and presence has disappeared. Individuals' mere existence is considered an effort that merits a reward. The click's instant reward alters social and moral principles. If mere presence grows into a legitimate claim for reward, then recognition is demanded (or guilt is assigned) not so much for ***doing*** something but rather for ***being*** somebody. This is not some political or cultural malfunction – this is the way a society built upon digital media has to be. We have yet to see the depths of this moral and social transformation.

Big implications of small efforts

Billions of users become accustomed to choosing smaller immediate rewards over larger delayed gratification. In psychology, such proclivity is associated with a deficit of self-control. Coupled with constantly produced but never satiating hits of micro-pleasure, this condition leads to a growing attachment to its source – what is more commonly known as digital addiction.

Those managing to avoid the risk of addiction do not escape the larger risk of critical detachment from physical reality. Adapting to the digital world alters the sensorium, diminishing the endurance, diligence, and resilience required to succeed in the physical world.

Technological development – from the use of fire to the invention of the hammer, the wheel, and the remote control (which was, for the sensorium, the prototype of a click) – has always sought to reduce the effort needed to receive rewards. The difference today is that the transition from the physical world to the digital world is happening with astonishing rapidity. The shift from nomadic to sedentary culture took millennia; the migration from villages to cities took centuries; the resettling of humankind onto the Internet will take about 70 years, starting in the 1980s with the introduction of the web.

In this period, humans will have to live in both physical and digital worlds. The older generations – digital immigrants – developed their basic physical skills before the Internet. Millennials, on the other hand, became the first digital natives. Starting with them, the physical, intellectual, and social development of individuals has been subjected to the pressure of the click's instant reward. Digital natives have grown up in an environment where rewards are not linked to significant effort but rather incentivize mere self-identification.

Interestingly, instead of the dichotomy of "digital natives" vs. "digital immigrants,"[1] there was a suggestion to use the terms "visitors" and "residents" as better descriptors of online engagement.[2] Indeed, younger generations reside in the digital world, while older generations merely visit

---

[1] Prensky, Marc. (2001). Digital Natives, Digital Immigrants. *On the Horizon*, MCB University Press, Vol. 9, No. 5, October.

[2] White, David S., and Le Cornu, Alison. (2011). Visitors and Residents: A new typology for online engagement. *First Monday*, 16(9).

it. However, the reverse is also true: digital residents only visit the physical world for some residual physical needs. And they always hurry to return to the digital environment, which is more comfortable for them due to its reward system. For them, digital residents, the slow and harsh physical reality requires too much effort. As more activities migrate online, digital natives increasingly withdraw from the physical world – the more disturbing part of their hybrid reality. The offline hesitancy of digital natives contributes to what is known as delayed adulthood: Millennials and the next generations have less or later sex, start fewer families, drive fewer cars, leave their parents' homes later (if at all), and so on.

Digital natives are becoming more physically and psychologically adapted to their new environment, but not to the old one. Coaches complain that kids are unable to firmly hold a hockey stick or do pull-ups. Their arms have been repurposed for manipulating digital devices, with the thumbs becoming operational fingers while losing their grip strength. Screens enhance tunnel vision – a digital native can see on-screen details that a digital immigrant cannot. As an "amputation" response (McLuhan), the peripheral vision of digital natives is deteriorating. Indeed, peripheral vision is redundant for screen use. But it is still required for safety in physical space.

When playing video games, digital immigrants instinctively dodge bullets or blows, but digital natives do not. Their bodies don't perceive an imaginary digital threat as a real one. Their sensorium has readjusted their bodies to ignore fake digital threats. There is no instinctive fear of heights or trauma in the digital world. Similarly, the fear of collision is cultivated by sports and physical activities, not by video games. In the digital world, even death can be overcome through re-spawning. What will happen when millions of young people with weakened grip strength, peripheral blindness, and no instinctive fear of collision start driving cars? Will media evolution be ready in time with its self-driving cars and self-driving everything?

Cultural settings are changing as well. Since clicks are so easy to perform, the exposure of people's presence to one another becomes enormous. The reward of recognition, promised by a click, gets lost in the incredible noise of all users' requests for affirmation. In the old physical world, people competed through the intensity of effort; in the new digital world, they compete through the intensity of their identity signals. Hence, the drift towards extreme opinions, outrage on social media, and political polarization is only natural in a society that rewards the intensity of self-identification more readily than it rewards efforts.

The click's instant reward renders any lasting effort, including long reading and even watching a long feature film, redundant and undesirable. The click's instant reward reshapes the structure of content packaging. The classic packaging of any content into the template of "exposition – climax – resolution," which used to be the structure of the completed narrative and hence of many organized activities, is becoming too time-consuming and bulky. In the past, linear reading of large, complete chunks of information might have required time and effort but helped develop rational, abstract, and deliberate thinking. This is being replaced with the flow of identity-signaling on Twitter and TikTok. Content used to be packed in complete parcels, such as books or stories; now it is packed into a flow – the news feed requiring endless scrolling.

The mainstream media hurry to warn that democracy is in danger, but these are the old democratic institutions and elites they worry about. In fact, never before has humankind had such an amount of democracy as now. It's not the lack of democracy but, quite the opposite, the oversupply of direct democracy that poses the real threat to the old democratic establishment. A child of the printing press, representative democracy, which was based on rational deliberation and institutions, collapses under the pressure of direct democracy based on digital torrents of instant identity signaling. The only survival strategy for the old establishment is to seize control of the latest form of social institutionalization – the digital platforms.

Recent social and political upheavals reflect this conflict between two subspecies of people whose sensorium, moral principles, and culture are based on either the delayed rewards offered by old media or instant rewards offered by new media. People familiar with the reward systems of both the physical world and digital reality can still differentiate between them, even when seduced into digital consumption. People who have experienced only digital rewards cannot. They tend to extend their digital reward expectations onto physical reality, demanding rewards for their mere existence/identity. Society is globally shifting from rewards for efforts to rewards for identity.

Media recapitulation

In 2014, Clay Shirky, a prominent new-media theorist, published an interesting reflection in the *Washington Post*[1] on his failed resistance to digital technology. For a long time, Shirky had allowed his students to use gadgets in class, thinking that banning the very subject he was studying would be embarrassing. He thought that a good professor teaching an interesting course could keep his students focused. But he realized that he could not. No lecture about the role of the telegraph during the Crimean War could rival a smartphone's flashing, vibrating notification that your ex just posted a new photo. He eventually gave up and banned the devices in the classroom.

Reflecting on his decision, Shirky tried to comfort himself, teachers, and parents, assuring that it was not their fault that they were losing their kids to gadgets. The entire tech industry – the entire process of media evolution – was working against them. New media recruit the best engineers, investors, scientists, and marketers to make their products more engaging. The only way to defeat gadgets in the fight for attention, he implied, is to ban them when attention is needed.

It seems that the conflict between reward systems makes digital distraction detrimental in activities that still require physical efforts. This presents a paradox we will likely have to deal with for another 40 or 50 years: should success in the physical world require curbing technologies that are otherwise essential in the digital world? And is that even doable? How can we abstain from digital media when everything around is becoming digital?

We have some idea about who is to blame. But what can be done?

The key to digital resistance lies not in neo-Luddism but in awareness of the media effects on our sensorium and our time. Media literacy is, first and foremost, time management. Media literacy is not just proficiency in using media; it is also the ability not to use media.

Digital detox is becoming a popular healthy lifestyle trend. Various digital detox services are promising for venture investment, and an entire industry is likely to emerge from this trend. But a digital detox regimen will

---

[1] Strauss, Valerie. (2014, September 25). Why a leading professor of new media just banned technology use in class. *The Washington Post*.

deal with a body already damaged by the Internet. To preserve the skills and functions still required in the physical world, it seems better to restrict, as regressive as it sounds, children's digital consumption while they develop the basic skills needed for the physical world.

In biology, there was a concept of biogenetic, or embryonic, recapitulation. The concept implies that "ontogeny recapitulates phylogeny" – the early development of an individual repeats the evolution of its species. For example, the human embryo develops features resembling gill arches, a tail, etc. Modern biology does not recognize recapitulation as a law, but this idea might provide a useful metaphor.

The principle of ***media recapitulation*** might be described as follows. To become a resourceful individual adapted to the modern reality of media consumption, a child has to go through all the basic stages of the species' media evolution through the oral, literate, print, and digital eras. Children, that is, should be taught step by step to manipulate toys, draw, read and write, and only then use electronic and digital media – strictly in that historically established order. The "individual" media evolution must repeat the stages of the media evolution of humankind sequentially. Exposure to next-stage media, if allowed prematurely, would interfere with mastering the earlier skills.

No rattle, coloring book, or adventure novel can compete with a digital device's instant reward. If newer media are introduced into a child's life before older media, they disturb the "evolutionary logic" of a child's sensory, mental, moral, and emotional development. If a child learns how to use a touchscreen before reading, the touchscreen's appeal and speed of reward will likely make this child a less able reader and a less diligent individual in general. It will be impossible to redirect the child's attention back to the book afterwards. The child's neurons will already be wired for an instant reward that no book can provide. Any attempt to teach children to use media with delayed rewards after they have already tried instant-reward media will likely lead to arguments, conflicts, and neuroses.

Just as media literacy means time management, media recapitulation essentially means age-based media access management. Responsible parents can identify the age ranges for giving children access to each new medium: playing with toys, listening to reading aloud, independent reading, TV, gadgets, video games, time-limited access to the Internet, and, eventually, unlimited access to the Internet with their own device. Media recapitulation will not solve the problem of the click's instant reward, but it could render constructive the essentially negative idea of digital prohibition. Media recapitulation turns prohibition into access – step-by-step access, based on the historical dynamic of media effects on humans' neurophysiology, sensorium, and social skills.

It is worth keeping in mind that the current stage of media evolution is not the final; it will be followed by media implanted into the body and later into the brain. Cognitive interfaces will become the last stage of human physical existence before our full resettling onto the Net. However, before that happens, two or three remaining generations will still have to live in the physical world and bear its risks, despite nearly complete digitalization.

Blissful ignorance

News avoidance is healthy for you, but bad for democracy and the media. Will AI be able to fix it?[1]

Walter Lippmann begins his 1922 book, Public Opinion, with a story about a small colony of Europeans living on a distant island, where a mail steamer delivered the news only once every 60 days. When the news arrived in September 1914, the colonists learned that, for over six weeks, those among them who were English and French had been at war with those who were Germans. A war had been consuming their home countries, but it would never have touched them if they had not received the news.

Unfortunately, Lippmann does not tell what happened to those people next. Did they turn from friends to enemies? Did they wish they'd been deprived of any news? They might have missed those days when they were still unaware of such bad news, as they were deprived of any news. For them, living without the latest news meant living without war.

Nowadays, what those colonists had by default due to the lack of communication has become the deliberate choice of many. It even has a name: "news avoidance."

News avoidance is at a historical high

News avoidance reached its peak in 2022, totaling 38% of all people globally and 42% of Americans, according to the 2022 Digital News Report by Reuters Institute.[2] The 2023 Digital News Report finds that globally, people most often avoid news about the war in Ukraine (39%), national

---

[1] The essay is based on the article with the same title in *Discourse*. (2023, December 14). Revised for book publication.

[2] Newman, Nic. (2022, June 15). Overview and key findings of the 2022 Digital News Report. *Reuters Institute*.

politics (38%), social justice issues (31%) and crime (30%).[1] In the U.S., the structure of selective news avoidance is slightly different, as shown in the chart (Figure 17).

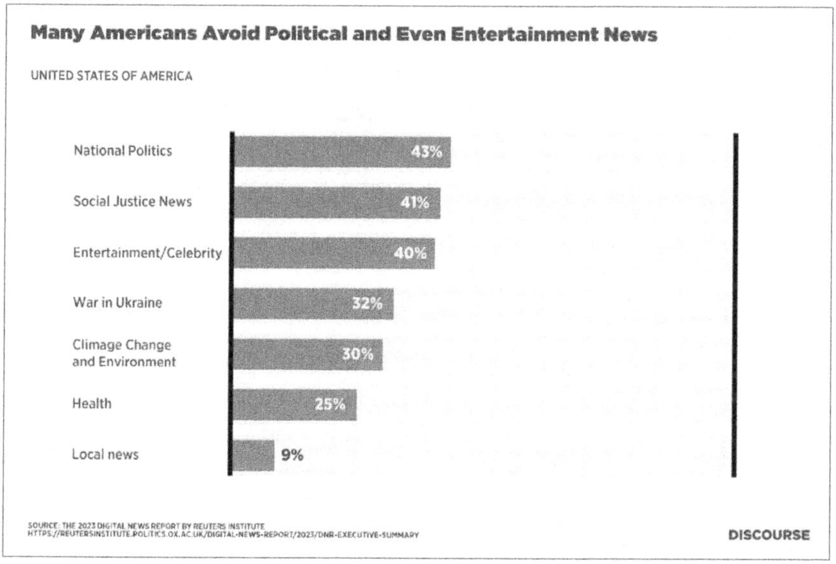

Figure 17. News avoidance in the U.S. according to the 2022 Digital News Report by Reuters Institute.[2] Image credit: Discourse.

In the U.S., the news people specifically avoid also reflects ideological preferences (Figure 18). Conservatives, for instance, are more likely to avoid news about social justice and climate change (70% and 64% respectively compared to 22% and 12% for liberals), while liberals are more likely to avoid news about crime and business (30% and 25% respectively compared to 14% and 9% for conservatives).

The term "news avoidance" first appeared in 1960, clearly coinciding with the TV boom. The next surge in news avoidance was related to the Internet. But news avoidance of the TV era and the early Internet was largely about news fatigue: people started experiencing information overload and therefore stopped watching or reading the news (Figure 19).

---

[1] Newman, Nic. (2023, June 14). Overview and key findings of the 2023 Digital News Report. *Reuters Institute*.

[2] Newman, Nic. (2022, June 15). Overview and key findings of the 2022 Digital News Report. *Reuters Institute*.

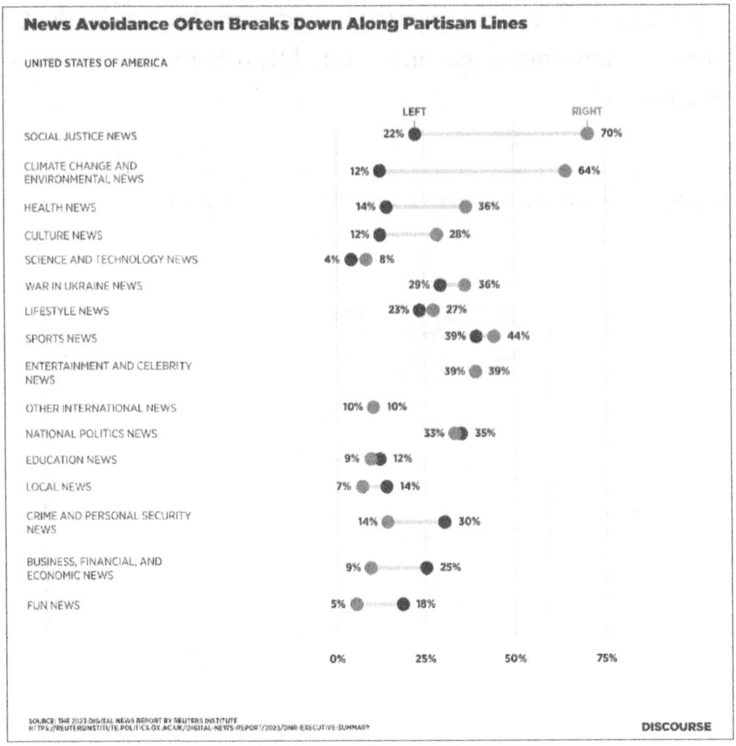

Figure 18. News avoidance: partisan division in the U.S. according to the 2022 Digital News Report by Reuters Institute.[1] *Image credit: Discourse.*

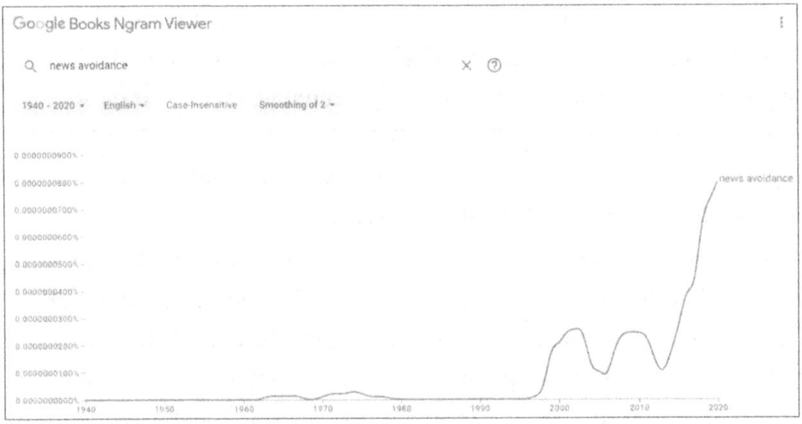

Figure 19. The frequency of using the term "news avoidance," according to Google Books Ngram.

[1] Newman, Nic. (2022, June 15). Overview and key findings of the 2022 Digital News Report. Reuters Institute.

The overload of negativity and the amputation of empathy

News fatigue can be explained through Marshall McLuhan's idea of sensory numbness. Electronic media has extended our nervous system to the entire planet. New forms of media have literally broadened our horizons but also opened us up to more stressors. Empathy, an essential element of humans' collective survival strategy, forces us to be attentive to the news about others, but TV and the Internet deliver too much of it. To protect the mind from informational and empathic overload, our news "receptors" become numb, which in turn results in the desire to avoid news.

If the early Internet oversupplied the amount of news, social media aggravated this overload by ramping up the emotional intensity of information. Since social media encourages engagement by triggering people's reactions, it heightened emotions and polarization. Legacy media followed suit, as it needed to compete for people's attention. As a result, regular-news overload has been upgraded to bad-news overload.

Why does bad news dominate so much of mass communication? We habitually blame journalists for all the "doom and gloom," but the media merely follow our own deep subliminal preferences. The simple truth is that people pay more attention to bad news than to good news. For example, as economists Daniel Kahneman and Amos Tversky show,[1] people prefer not to lose $5 over finding $5. To put it another way, the desire to avoid negative consequences is much stronger than the desire for positive outcomes. This negativity bias represents a survival strategy too and serves as a warning system about potential threats. This is why we instinctively value negative information more than positive information. So, all the "doom and gloom" in the media is based on our subliminal preferences, fostered by evolution.

Nowadays, however, the amalgamation of this negativity bias with the news overload through the Internet and social media has created the perfect storm of global news insanity. The more this storm rages, the more

[1] See: Kahneman, Daniel, and Tversky, Amos. (1979). Prospect theory: An analysis of decision under risk. *Econometrica*, 47(2), pp. 263–291.

people think the world is going crazy. For instance, they feel that wars, atrocities and catastrophes are occurring at historically high rates. But this is not true; it's a media effect rather than a historic phenomenon; or rather a historic phenomenon caused by a media effect.

There have always been wars and atrocities, and often they have been much worse than what we're seeing today. The difference is that the news of today's wars and atrocities is now delivered directly to each of us on individual screens, involving people personally – even driving some to street rallies and making overseas wars into local incidents, which was simply impossible before news media.

Observing the effect of television, McLuhan posited that the emotional perception of TV replaces the rational detachment typical of print culture. Unlike books, electronic media provoke the "empathic involvement" natural to tribal unity; McLuhan called this effect the "retribalization" of society. McLuhan's retribalization has merged with the global village and given birth to global tribalism. Moreover, the expectation of this global tribal reaction provokes even more those who perpetrate atrocities – they benefit from the global empathic reaction. For them, carnage is the medium that is meant to be the message. Global empathic involvement, fostered by electronic and now digital media, makes terrorism more efficient than war – especially for those who have no resources to fight a full-scale war. And the primary medium of violence becomes not a gun but a smartphone. This media effect both "invites" terrorism and saturates the media agenda with violence – in addition to the agonistic tone inherent in social media.[1]

Not everyone, of course, can withstand the agitation produced by such a media environment. Some lose empathy and become cynical. Others try to fence off their empathy by avoiding bad news and, eventually, the news in general.

After reaching its peak in 2022, the news avoidance trend seemed to stabilize in 2023, signaling, perhaps, that we're reaching a new balance between empathy and news disturbance. But it is likely a temporary pause. Now, after the recent Hamas terrorist attack and Israel's war on terror in Gaza, news avoidance will surely rise further.

[1] I explored the polarizing effects of new and old media in 2020 *Postjournalism and the Death of Newspapers. The Media after Trump: Manufacturing Anger and Polarization*.

War news in general is one of the main causes of news avoidance. This may be especially true in countries close to the conflict, as has been the case in those nations located near the war in Ukraine, according to the Reuters report. But even in distant countries, war news might become the last straw in people's informational and emotional news overload. The Israel-Hamas war may be thousands of miles away, but the news, much like that mail steamer in Lippmann's story, brought it to the American and European streets and campuses, agitating some people while numbing the news receptors of others.

The media are trapped in a bad-news cycle and so is their audience. Most bad news is repeated constantly, emotionally draining the readers, viewers and listeners. "When we ask people why they are actively avoiding news, they're saying a few key things: they are put off by the repetitiveness of the news agenda, they feel worn out, and they feel that the news is bad for their mental health," says Kirsten Eddy, a researcher at the Reuters Institute.[1] People might be sympathetic, but since they can change nothing, they feel helplessness, anxiety or anger. Most frustrating, perhaps, is not even the news itself but the reactions of others who get it "wrong." This is the so-called third-person effect. Everybody thinks that everyone else but me is easily deluded by the media and propaganda.

Bad-news cycles don't just put us in a bad mood, they create a psychological issue that threatens to grow into a psychiatric one. Psychologists advise us to remind ourselves that unlike 20 years ago, we are now our own gatekeepers and can control our news consumption. Among the practical tips of media hygiene is turning off news notifications or even all pop-up notifications, limiting our responses on social media, and so on. Since the survival mechanism of attention to negative news itself became a threat, many tips on media hygiene basically lead to news avoidance, adding a clear rationale to what people already feel instinctively.

No pain no gain: News avoidance blinds the public

But what is good for mental health is not so healthy for democracy. News avoidance reduces civic engagement. In the classical liberal view, democracy is based on a well-informed citizenry. Obviously, if 40% of

---

[1] News avoidance and why it matters. *News Over Noise podcast*, News Literacy Initiative, Pennstate.

citizens avoid news, many will not be well-informed. By eschewing frustrating news topics, people also avoid discussing them publicly. Thus, news avoidance also leads to a form of self-censorship.

News avoidance obviously harms the news industry. Since negative information is evolutionarily more valuable for humans, the news media are naturally tuned into negativity bias. As the old newspaper saying goes, "If it bleeds, it leads." But if "it bleeds" too much, it leads to a disaster – both for society and the media.

Meanwhile, people in the news industry have been discussing if it is possible to build a successful media outlet without negativity bias. Most suggestions revolve around different models of "constructive journalism," "solution journalism," or "slow journalism." And indeed, surveys show that people say they would read positive and uplifting news. However, this is what people always say but never do.

A project of "constructive" or "solution" journalism might be lucky enough to secure funding, but it will never garner an audience sufficient to sustain the project itself, not to mention making a social impact. "Solution" journalism might solve the problem of the limited number of journalists through securing philanthropic funding for them, but it cannot resolve the environmental problem of negativity experienced by readers, the industry, and society.

Furthermore, attempts to eradicate negativity from journalism are not just unfeasible – they are inherently wrong. Negativity in the news is as crucial as pain is to the body, signaling important issues. Moreover, just as with pain, it's not only the negativity but also the volume of negativity that holds meaning. The more people are agitated, the more significant the issue is.

Of course, negativity and mass agitation can be artificially created or stirred up by malicious politicians to advance their careers, by media to drum up business, or by the very design of social media, which is aimed at boosting engagement. Perhaps, it is exactly this "added value" of negativity that drives the audience's frustration and, ultimately, its news avoidance.

Nevertheless, even this excessive negativity is indicative of what stressors and the means of their delivery agitate society the most. Eliminating this pain will make society unaware of its issues, whether political or communicative. How else can society learn about issues with education, healthcare, the party system, or border security if not just a few, but many are discussing them? The amount of pain – of social frustration caused by the news – matters. It should be sensed by the public and politicians for curative actions to be taken. News avoidance eliminates this source of public awareness.

How could AI fix it?

It turns out that the factors that cause news avoidance simultaneously represent the greatest value of news for society. Is it possible to alleviate pain while preserving its indicative function? Theoretically, this could be a job for AI, when the tools of semantic and sentiment analysis become affordable enough to be repurposed for mass media.

Alleviating the emotional burden for the end user while measuring and indicating the range and structure of societal agitation can be achieved programmatically. Special apps could offer readers the option to regulate their personally bearable level of empathic exposure or receive only a summary of emotional measurements – similar to the summaries of news and public opinion that politicians and business leaders receive from their analysts to gauge the national mood. This way, AI that measures the scale of negativity and the structure of societal agitation would mediate not news itself but agitation induced by news, potentially shielding those who are empathetic and often avoid the news due to emotional overload.

It is hard to say if a significant number of news avoiders would willingly and routinely consume news, emotionally refined by AI, but some might. Instead of media selectively omitting one stressor while amplifying others and thus adding to news frustration even more, such an automated solution would make a user a true gatekeeper – not only for the news but for its emotional impact, too. Of course, it will work only until the algorithms of such emotional mediation are tweaked, too. But this will be the story of media bias of the next level.

Past their prime (time)

Fox News and CNN enter the last stage of their parallel history[1]

There is some accidental symbolism in the concurrent ousting of Don Lemon from CNN and Tucker Carlson from Fox News. Despite the different weights of these talents for their outlets, their firing opens what may be the last chapter in the histories of both of the greatest American TV networks. Carlson's and Lemon's departures are certainly headline-worthy – particularly that of Carlson, who's been a main driver of Fox News' primetime viewership. But what really matters for the media is the future fate of CNN, Fox News, and TV news in general – and it's not a pretty picture. Indeed, it's even uncertain whether they do have viable paths for survival.

CNN and Fox News often mirrored each other at various points in their journeys. The latest twist in their parallelism relates to the plans of CNN's new leadership,[2] which has recently been accused of intending to transform CNN into another Fox News. The reason was that the new bosses claimed to steer away from "partisan and alarmist programming in favor of neutral journalism and balanced debate."[3] They were immediately blamed for "both-siding democracy."[4] A funny fact: from 1992 to 2000, CNN produced a show called "Both Sides with Jesse Jackson". Presenting both sides was once a virtue on CNN. Now, as people in the media know, bothsidesism is a major sin in journalism, a slippery slope towards Fox News (as if Fox News both-sides anything).

In fact, CNN had already been like Fox News – not ideologically, of course, but morphologically, as a politicized type of television.

---

[1] The essay is based on the article with the same title in *Discourse*. (2023, April 26). Revised for book publication.

[2] Martin Gurri. The Fifth Wave: CNN's long goodbye. *Discourse*.

[3] Fischer, Sara. (2022, July 21). Scoop: CNN boss' Capitol Hill diplomacy tour. *Axios*.

[4] Klein, Charlotte. (2022, September 7). "I really hope that we don't both-sides democracy": where is CNN headed? *Vanity Fair*.

On the origin of species

In biology, the concept of convergent evolution explains why different species can develop similar features despite belonging to different classes of animals or plants. For example, sharks and dolphins belong to fishes and mammals, respectively, and they have nothing in common biologically. However, living in the same environmental niche, they eventually developed similar physical characteristics. It was ecological conditions, not biological kinship, that gave them fins and made their bodies similar, even though they remain natural "antagonists."

It turns out that convergent evolution can tell us just as much about the media landscape. CNN is 16 years older than Fox News – the networks were founded in 1980 and 1996, respectively. They emerged in different eras of TV technologies, and this technological and historical gap shaped their initially different approaches to journalism. But as with sharks and dolphins, the media environment has eventually turned CNN and Fox News into two specimens that look very much alike.

In the late 1970s, CNN founder Ted Turner led the wave of technological innovation that enabled 24/7 TV news coverage. As always happens when a new medium emerges that delivers information faster, from much farther away, or in a new format, the public wanted more news of this amazing kind. By the 1980s, the technologies of electronic news gathering replaced film cameras and video cassettes. The speed of news production increased exponentially. On-the-scene satellite transmission made news trucks another technological breakthrough. Live streaming started shaping the news habits of the TV audience. In response, the demand for "raw" news grew. In such conditions, journalism of facts inevitably dominates. CNN became the new TV medium that shaped and satisfied the demand for "raw" facts.

The young and ambitious network became nationally renowned after the space shuttle Challenger disaster in January 1986. As hard as it might be to believe today, CNN was the only national news broadcaster covering the launch live. The shock of the tragedy was tremendously amplified, of course, by a media effect – by the effect of "happening right now" innate to live TV. This was perhaps the first media catastrophe of this kind and scale – a live-TV catastrophe, followed by rolling news coverage for hours and days.

Before the Challenger disaster, CNN had struggled to figure out its mission and place. But "after this coverage, I rarely had to explain to people what CNN was," recalled a staffer.[1] A new quality of news was tasted and accepted by millions. Ted Turner gained the reputation of a man who "transformed viewers in 150 countries into 'instant witnesses of history.'" [2]

The format reached its pinnacle in January 1991, during the Gulf War when CNN covered the airstrike in Baghdad. This was the first war televised live. Sadly, live news reporting soon made the public way more present in the sights of mass deaths, which culminated, of course, in the live TV coverage of the 9/11 attacks, when the tragedy unfolded right before viewers' eyes.

Milestone events – from the 1986 Challenger disaster to the 1991 Gulf War to the 9/11 terrorist attacks – fully revealed the strength of the live news streaming. Live, objective reporting became CNN's product and creed – and it stayed that way for more than a decade and a half. The format truly transformed TV journalism. The focus on the immediacy of the picture – on the "presence effect" – enforced the ethos of objectivity in reporting. Commentary was reserved for pundits in the studio. Most importantly, judgment was left to viewers.

The user becomes the content

The success of CNN in 24/7 news programming generated numerous imitations and increased the prominence of live news reporting on TV. But soon, it became apparent that the medium's capacity to deliver 24/7 news surpassed the world's ability to provide 24/7 events. News streaming without events became boring, even pointless. News streaming with events became overwhelming and required guidance, when was conducted by many. A demand and a market for commentaries and explanations emerged.

This is what caused the simultaneous launch of Fox News and MSNBC in 1996. Both emulated the rolling news cycle but emphasized longer stories with more extensive details and extended commentaries, aimed

---

[1] Escobedo, Tricia. (2016, March 31). "When a national disaster unfolded live in 1986." CNN.

[2] Guthey, Eric. (1997). "Ted Turner's media legend and the transformation of corporate liberalism." Business and Economic History, Fall 1997, Vol. 26, No. 1, pp. 184-199.

more at attracting viewers than at reflecting the news. News coverage became dependent not only on what was happening, but also on what the audience wanted to see.

In part, it also was a by-product of the new technologies that allowed networks to measure the viewership and see the characteristics of the audience for better advertising. Since the magic of 24/7 news coverage began fading, a new focus of TV production emerged – the audience's social demographics. As media theorist Marshall McLuhan once predicted, the user became the content. News was abundant, and the audience needed guidance; guidance is always more attentive to the audience's characteristics than news.

Thus, the technological changes that enhanced and accelerated the supply of "raw" news first favored journalism of facts; but when oversupplied, "raw" news eventually increased the demand for opinion journalism.

Such a dynamic of relations between new technologies, market saturation, and journalism has a curious ethical implication. Journalism of facts sees professional dignity in unbiased mediation and supplying data for people to make their own conclusions. Therefore, journalism of facts recognizes the agency of the public; it treats the audience as adults who can take in information and make their own judgments. Opinion journalism, on the other hand, responds to the need for guidance and navigation. Seduced into shepherding, opinion journalism tends to treat the audience as children and ends up, eventually, in preaching.

In a media ecosystem in which journalism of facts dominates, the public is seen as able, curious, responsible and smart. But in a media ecosystem dominated by opinion journalism, the public is seen as dependent, fragile, deceived and, frankly, stupid. It is expected that someone authoritative and morally capable must step in to tell the audience right from wrong.

Anyway, CNN and Fox News were different by virtue of their origins. If, on CNN, Ted Turner televised the telegraph, then Roger Ailes, on Fox News, completed the making of television. Ailes refocused TV production from news supply to viewers' attraction. He fully unveiled the specific and unique capacity of TV: the delivery of an affirmative emotional world picture talking to the viewers at their homes and within their value systems.

Being more audience-centered than news-centered, both Fox News and MSNBC spearheaded the shift from objectivity to subjectivity in covering news. News anchors stopped being presenters and became news shepherds, guiding their audiences to conclusions. Giving more air to commentaries and opinions, both new networks, Fox News and MSNBC, drifted toward more political engagement. As networks designed for more political commentary, Fox News and MSNBC started outperforming CNN in attracting audiences in the conditions of news abundance, especially with the growing role of the Internet in news supply. But among all three, Fox News happened to be a better fit for what came next.

The last mutation

The Internet gave everyone access to content production and delivery. Blogs enabled anyone to be a published writer. Social media made everyone accidental reporters and commentators. As a result, everyone, from corporations and public figures to ordinary people, became the media on their own. As opposed to the Challenger disaster in 1986, the loss of the space shuttle Columbia in 2003 was not just televised[1] by three 24-hour cable networks – CNN, Fox News and MSNBC – but also covered via the Internet.

By the 2010s, traditional media had lost its monopoly over the news, commentary and even the "presence effect". A new medium, the Internet, provided oversupply of not just news but everything – any kind of content. The pendulum between journalism of facts and opinion journalism not just swayed – it got broken.

The media were confused, and they reacted within the old paradigm: they responded to the oversupply of content with even more "guidance," having rapidly grown into "adults" talking to children. In 2013, Pew Research Center[2] looked at the ratio between news and opinion content on the leading cable news networks and found that 85% of MSNBC's content was opinion, compared with 15% news. On CNN, factual reporting was slightly over half of content production, but, generally, the overall ratio between news and opinions was already close to that of Fox News.

---

[1] Escobedo, Tricia. (2016, March 31). "When a national disaster unfolded live in 1986." *CNN*.

[2] The changing TV news landscape. (2013, March 17). *Pew Research Center*.

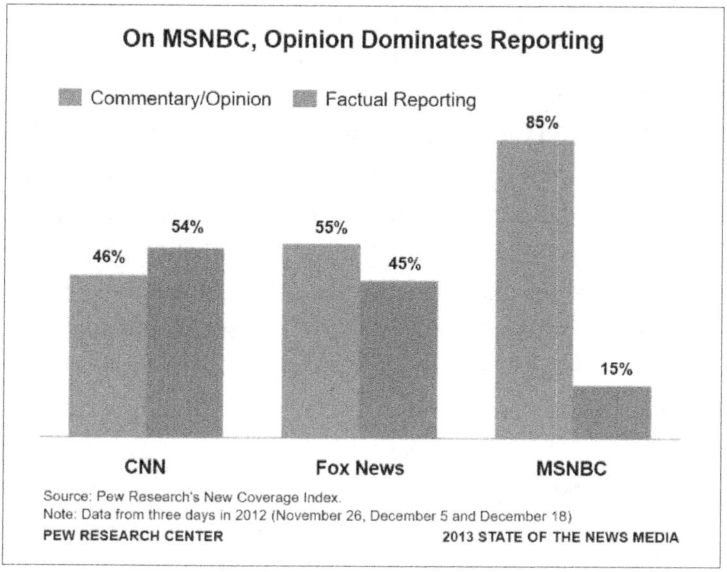

Figure 20. Data: 2013 State of the News Media, Pew Research Center.[1]

This happened long before the political rise of Donald Trump. Because of the Internet, the ecology of news shifted dramatically, changing journalism and thus modifying the ways society spoke about its issues. A massive study of news presentation over the past 30 years, conducted by the RAND Corporation[2] in 2018, revealed that broadcast journalism – non-cable TV news like CBS, NBC and ABC – after 2000 lost its former adherence to precise and concrete language and increased the share of "unplanned speech, expression of opinions, interviews, and arguments." Even more dramatic changes happened to journalism in cable news: prime-time cable news became based more "on the expression of opinion than on the provision of facts" and more likely offered "advocacy for those same opinions rather than a balanced description of context or events."

The massive increase of subjectivity in cable news as compared to broadcast news came from the business model. Cable news financially relied not only on ads but also on bundle subscription. As the RAND study says, this made cable news even more "opinion-oriented than broadcast

---

[1] The changing TV news landscape. (2013, March 17). Pew Research Center.

[2] Kavanagh, Jennifer, et al. (2018). How the style and language of news presentation is changing in the digital age. RAND Corporation.

news in order to appeal to specific niche audiences." Therefore, cable news presenters became more inclined than their broadcast counterparts to be advocates and guides for their niche audiences.

For Fox News and MSNBC, politicization was natural, as it strengthened ties with their niche audiences. However, for CNN, the politicization that followed its niche specialization delivered the final and deadly blow to the fact-reporting approach to news. CNN suffered the same changes that affected all 20th-century classical journalism after digitalization. Since the audience and ads moved online, the media began wooing the digital audience. It was the early years of social media, and the digital public consisted predominantly of educated and progressive urbanites. The media strived to earn the favor of this audience and aligned with its values.

This is how CNN found a new reference group to appeal to, after already being dragged from factual reporting into opinion journalism. The issue, however, was that digital users did not need TV to inform them. Even worse, advertisers were aware of it – they dramatically decreased ad budgets in traditional media. From the perspective of the media business, targeting progressive digital audiences became a trap that CNN remains ensnared in, despite the latest changes in leadership.

Enter Trump

Not long ago, the mainstream media were often accused of "hidden liberal bias." They rejected it and insisted on their unbiased reporting and objective journalism, the most neutral and therefore suitable vehicle for advertising. After the media lost ad revenue and stuck to digital progressives, any accusations of "hidden liberal bias," as well as the denial of such accusations, became pointless.

However, this rapid and massive progressive shift in news coverage caused backlash among conservatives. By the mid-2010s, their use of social media had grown big enough to accumulate their grievances into a significant political force. Thus emerged Donald Trump.

The news media quickly learned to profit on the validation of Trump as a threat to democracy. In doing so, the media, of course, fell into the temptation of not only validating but also producing disturbing news for its further recycling. No matter how much they warned each other not to be obsessed with Trump, they simply could not stop reporting on him. This last business convulsion strengthened the ties of most news media to the progressives and, basically, turned the media into hostages of the Twitterati, who demanded loyalty but never rewarded it, while always punishing disloyalty – a classic of abusive relationships.

Under the pressure of the Internet, journalism rapidly mutated into postjournalism: dependence on digital audiences, rather than on advertisers, led the mainstream media to switch from news supply to news validation.[1] Postjournalism was not a big deal for Fox News. Because the network focused on opinion journalism from the start, its acceptance of news validation instead of news reporting was organic. Postjournalism, however, has completely redesigned the rest of the mainstream media – they had farther to move on the road from facts to opinion than Fox News did. But they have caught up.

The environmental deadlock

Can CNN reverse "my-side boosterism" and be forced back to "objective" reporting? Technically, yes: the restoring of unbiased news reporting and all-sides consideration are simple professional tasks, and there are still a lot of people around who remember how to do that. But will this save CNN? No.

The task to restore objectivity and fact-based reporting on CNN is what Marshall McLuhan called the "rear-view mirror" consciousness: moving forward while looking back at the rear-view mirror. The type of journalism that the new leadership of CNN supposedly wants to restore disappeared not because of malevolence or negligence of the past leadership, but because the conditions for that kind of journalism had disappeared. It was the environment, not someone's will or conspiracy, that turned CNN into an opinionated media outlet. To reverse the mutation of CNN, one would need to reverse the evolution of the entire media environment. Good luck with that.

The issue is that the crucial shift occurred not on the side of news production but on the side of news consumption. One can decorate a

---

[1] I developed the concept of postjournalism in *Postjournalism and the Death of Newspapers. The Media after Trump: Manufacturing Anger and Polarization* (2020).

phaeton with whatever luxury features imaginable, but personal transportation has already shifted to the Ford Model T. The new media habits do not and will not favor pre-programmed TV watching tied to the schedule of newsroom, not viewer. People want to watch what they want and when they want – not what and when TV orgs want them to watch. News now has better formats and channels for delivery to users. Advertisers have access to much cheaper and more efficient platforms for delivering customized visual messaging.

There is some residual TV business remaining, but it is tied to a certain social demographic that is already mostly owned by Fox News. This older social demographic has largely held onto its TV consumption habits and will continue to do so until the last people of the last TV generation hold the last remote controls in their hands. But beyond this social demographic and its habits, TV news is already losing its industrial scale. This process, known as cord-cutting, has little to nothing to do with the quality of news or journalism; it's an environmental change.

The generational shift in media platforms is accompanied and exacerbated by the generational shift in the audience. The demand for objective journalism primarily comes from those who want to disseminate, not consume it (who remember the social function of journalism and value it). All the rest, who could consume news, are increasingly seduced by other media habits and don't really care if journalism is objective, subjective, or even exists at all. Therefore, the only viable business model for objective journalism is to be financially supported "from above" – by those who want this noble kind of journalism to survive and be delivered to others. But "others" don't care.

The paradox is that objective, middle-ground, adult-conversation journalism can be produced but cannot be consumed at the scale sufficient to support TV production. It is technically possible to restore high-quality objective TV journalism; this could even secure a prominent place in someone's media diet. But it will always rely on life support, not on the market.

Amidst this tectonic shift, the departure of star news anchors is a relatively insignificant event, yet it's definitely a symbolic one. It represents the last chapters in the historical parallelism of CNN and Fox News. While the networks were founded in different technological eras with different professional creeds, they became similar as they lived through the same climate changes that converged their journalistic approaches. The only difference between CNN and Fox News that matters is the difference between their demographics. The social demographic of Fox News remains, and will remain for some time, more loyal to the habits of classical TV watching in its last form: an affirmative and emotional picture of the world delivered in the fashion of scheduled broadcasting. But this demographic resource is limited anyway: old TV habits will be gone with the last TV generation. As for objective journalism, it was gone when the media – CNN included – were forced to chase the audience running away to digital. The prime time of primetime news is truly over.

The platform paradox

We can grow our digital "bodies" – but we cannot own them[1]

In their first decade, Internet services from Google to Facebook to Twitter insisted that they were neutral platforms designed to serve users. The users, not the platforms, would choose what to post or read online; the users, not the platforms, would retain ultimate control over what they decided to say or do.

That Internet ceased to exist on January 8, 2021, when the tech companies banished former president Donald Trump and many of his supporters from their platforms. After this, the platforms got caught in a peculiar sort of regulatory capture. They tightened control over users because they feared stricter regulation, as their previous "neutrality" was blamed for the political disturbances in 2016 and 2021. At the same time, by banning none other than the president and eradicating wrong agendas, the platforms proved how powerful they are and thus only spurred the public and deep state's appetite for regulatory intervention.

As a result, digital platforms evolved from content neutrality to meticulous control over users' behavior. Deciding to censor their users at scale, they struck an unusual alliance with state agencies, academic centers, and anti-"misinformation" nonprofits that the investigative journalists who uncovered the "Twitter Files" have aptly labeled the "censorship-industrial complex."[2]

But lurking behind the digital free-speech debate are fundamental questions of digital rights. Who owns our content, our accounts, or the digital personas we cultivate? If a platform can ban a president, it can do anything to anyone. Who, then, should protect users' digital rights, civic and consumerist, against platforms that expropriate everything users

---

[1] The essay is based on the article with the same title in *City Journal* (2024, Summer). Revised for book publication.

[2] Stern, Seth. (2023, March 16). Congressional hearing on Twitter Files shows why conservatives need the PRESS Act. *Freedom of the Press Foundation*.

create on them? We have entered a new political-economic situation in which digital civic rights and the rights of digital property are not yet fully established, while traditional concepts of political freedoms and property rights increasingly fail online. To establish a coherent framework of digital rights, we need to understand the nature of the modern platform economy. What, exactly, do platforms produce that gives them such power?

How to sell air

Imagine you have some Nothing – pure, unalloyed Nothing – that you have decided to sell on Amazon or eBay. Imagine further that, because of some glitch, the selling platform shows your offer to 10 million users. Some people would buy that Nothing, either by mistake or out of curiosity. With a good conversion rate, you've got good revenue. If the glitch shows your offer of Nothing to a billion users, you'll be a millionaire.

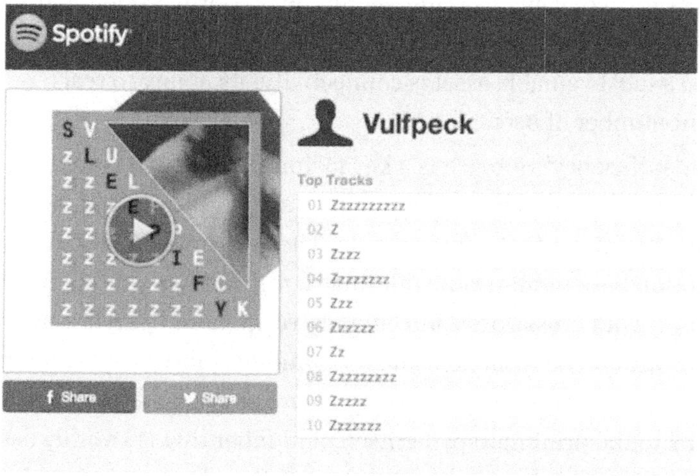

Figure 21. The playlist of Vulfpeck's album Sleepify.

This scenario is no fantasy. In 2014, the funk band Vulfpeck from Ann Arbor, Michigan, posted on Spotify a new album, *Sleepify*, that contained ten tracks of silence (Figure 21). They asked fans to stream the songs on a loop, which would allow the band to collect royalties of one-half of a cent for each stream to crowdfund an upcoming free concert tour.[1] Their fans

[1] Gensler, Andy. (2014, April 4). Vulfpeck stands to earn more than $18k from Spotify for silent album. Billboard.

responded enthusiastically, and the story went viral. In a month, the blank tracks were played over 5 million times, earning[1] the band about $20,000. Spotify tolerated the gambit for a while but then took the album down.

Using this surplus value of the platform's reach in a slightly different way, two Canadians from sunny Alberta became merchants of air. They put a Ziploc bag of air on eBay, and somebody bought it for 99 cents. They lost money on shipping but got an idea.[2] They started compressing crisp Albertan air into cans and selling it abroad, reaching $300,000 in annual sales in 2018 through online purchases and retail stores in South Korea, where Canadian air is perhaps considered particularly sweet. They say that if they hit the retail market in China or India, sales will be in the millions. Of course, this kind of reach works even when you sell air.

These light stories suggest a heavier lesson. Despite Bill Gates's proclamation in 1996, content is no king on the Internet. Instead, ***reach*** is king. With enough reach, one can sell anything – even air or silence.

A new form of value has emerged in the platform economy. It has little to do with exchange-value, use-value, or the concept of a commodity. A platform's most valuable asset is connectivity: its ability to reach a sufficient number of users.

The "sufficiency" of reach is a key factor: one needs to surpass a certain threshold of reach to achieve the platform effect. This is what the New York Times is attempting to do, for example. They try anything to increase the subscription base numerically: offering significant entry discounts, luring subscribers with crosswords and culinary recipes, and purchasing the sports news site The Athletic with its 1.2 million subscribers – anything to boost the "platform reach." In the meantime, only about 700,000 people subscribe to the print newspaper itself, a number that is steadily declining. Digital-news-only subscribers sit at 3 million[3], representing less than one-third of total subscribers. Yet the Times is successfully expanding its total reach, clearly aiming to evolve into a platform business. The company initially set out to have 10 million subscribers by 2025; it hit this target in 2023 and is now pursuing a "meaningfully larger number."[4] After building

---

[1] Sleepify. Wikipedia.

[2] Fletcher, Robson. (2019, April 6). Here's how 2 guys from Alberta are selling $300K worth of canned air a year. CBC.

[3] The New York Times Company Reports. Third-Quarter 2023 Results.

[4] Hirsh, Lauren, Draper, Kevin, and Rosman Katherine. (2022, January 6). New York

a sufficiently large platform, the Times will be able to sell anything content-related it wants.

Reach is what matters: the commodity for sale is of secondary importance. Platform reach constitutes a new asset whose value exceeds the value of the underlying content. The medium is the message: for the platform as the medium, the message is reach.

In the case of the New York Times, the question is where the threshold of sufficient reach in this niche is. What is the subscribership size that will turn the former newspaper into a niche platform? Is 10–15 million enough to sell anything content-related, including the compressed air of the newsroom?

Another issue is retaining subscribers. Social media, Google, and e-commerce platforms such as eBay or Amazon have natural attractors. People "organically" go there for their essential needs: socialization, search, shopping. The New York Times has no such natural attractors for a sufficient number of people to stay or return. Operational costs for retaining millions of reluctant users can become a critical issue. Nevertheless, the New York Times is the only traditional mainstream media outlet trying to enter the platform business in their niche. All the rest keep struggling with selling news and ads, which is hopeless, as news is free online, and ads work incomparably better on platforms, not in the media.

The four corollaries to the network effect

So, platform reach is a new product whose value can exceed or even completely replace the value of content. How can we define this platform surplus value?

Theoretically, there is a formula for it, and it is called the "network effect." The network effect is described by Metcalfe's law: the value of a network is proportional to the square of the number of networked users.[1] In other words, the more users that participate, the more connections they form, and the more each of them benefit from those connections.

A good illustration of the network effect was offered by Clay Shirky in his 2010 book *Cognitive Surplus*. Suppose you want a ride to New Jersey at

---

Times Co. to buy the Athletic for $550 million in cash. *The New York Times*.

[1] Metcalfe's law. *Wikipedia*.

a certain time and post a request on a car-sharing service. If, after making 20 such requests, you find only a few takers, you'll probably decide not to use the service again. The network effect was not achieved. But if you get 18 matches, the service is good. For this to happen, the service must attract all possible riders in the area. Then, you will likely find any matches you need. Somebody will drive at the needed time to the needed place.

Out of this, we can derive...

The 1st corollary to Metcalfe's law: The best platform is a monopolistic platform.

If all the users gather on a single platform, all the possible matches between them will occur. We will benefit the most from only one Facebook, only one Google, only one Amazon, only one Twitter/X, only one Tinder, only one carsharing service. Any split (except for niche specializations, of course) will diminish the network effect and therefore the platform surplus value for us users.

This is similar to the swarming effect: the larger the swarm, the more likely individuals are to join. The viral effect works in the same manner: the bigger the viral distribution, the likelier it is that users will join and contribute to it, making it even bigger, proving its significance, and providing delivery to an even larger number of users. The network effect naturally drives platforms toward monopolization – not due to the evil will of the platform overlords (though they like it, too), but through the activity of the users if the users are pleased by the outcomes of connectivity.

The monopolization of a platform maximizes the network effects but also raises the risks associated with any monopoly, including political and policy abuses, as well as potential technical glitches – akin to the 2003 northeast power blackout caused by a software bug. Political and policy abuses, theoretically, could be overseen by regulation, but the regulation of platforms carries its own political risks, as shown by the Twitter Files.

Platform monopolization has natural limits tied to generational changes. New digital features or new generations of users arrive and undermine old monopolies. For example, MySpace was the first social media platform to reach a global audience, but then Facebook offered more advanced features and made MySpace obsolete. Twitter, Instagram, and TikTok also offered specific networking features and established a monopoly in their niches.

At the same time, all platforms seek not just niche monopoly but also universality. They consistently try to add new features to capture as many users' activities as possible. It is conceivable, therefore, that niche platforms' monopolies can be challenged by a super-monopoly. In this case, the universal, ultimate social media platform will eventually emerge that will embody all the possible features of social networking – from chatting and dating to video posting and digital shopping. So far, WeChat might be the closest to this universal social media platform.

The dependency of users' benefit on the largest possible reach leads to...

The 2nd corollary to Metcalfe's law: in the ideal network, any possible matches become inevitable.

Say you want to have a cup of coffee with someone near Times Square at 5pm and post an invite on Facebook. If you have 200 Facebook friends, the offer probably won't be taken up. But if you have 5,000 friends and 20,000 followers, the cafeteria will not fit all those seeking to have a chat with you. In this case, people will not just statistically-accidentally coincide with you; they will ***want*** to coincide.

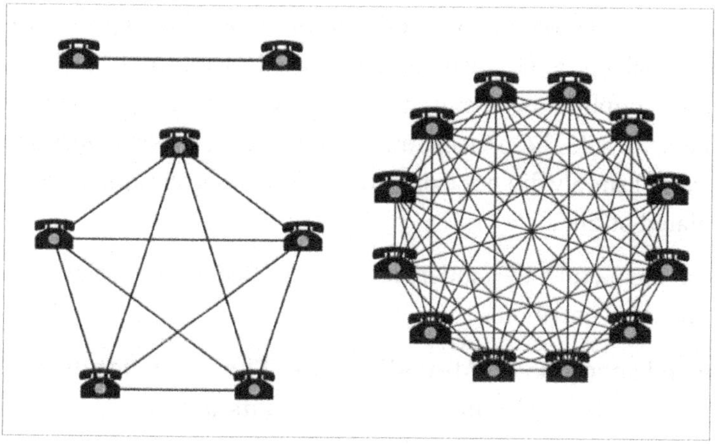

Figure 22. Metcalf suggested his law for connected devices. When humans connect, they are proactive; they create additional gravitational forces within their networks of connections. Image credit: based on an image from Wikimedia Commons.[1]

[1] Metcalfe's law. Wikipedia.

Robert Metcalfe introduced his law for a network of devices, such as fax machines or telephones (Figure 22). When the networked nodes are humans, the ***statistical*** network effect turns into a ***social*** network effect. Humans amplify connectivity by their proactive attitudes towards each other – for better or worse. They seek to coincide – to resonate with each other, especially with those capable of creating significant resonance themselves, such as celebrities and authoritative figures.

The size of one's social graph – all a person's connections on a platform – reflects not just numbers but also a person's social capital. People in one's social graph, or within one's platform reach, are those who are interested in this person or in what interests this person. Social capital is the surplus of people who know a person over the number of people this person knows. When this surplus is significant, a person can capitalize on his or her personality in all possible ways, from professional to hobbyist, recreational, or partner-matching. This person can sell air and songs of silence.

Platforms facilitate social "capitalism" incredibly well. On top of the human-driven viral/swarming effect, algorithms calculate who might like whom or what, and then they amplify outreach by adjusting what to show to whom. Social pro-activity of interconnected users, amplified by algorithms, amplifies even more the network effect and social capital of everyone involved. These mechanisms of the network and algorithmic amplification simply did not exist when people's social capital was accumulated offline.

Social media turn the statistical network effect into a social network effect, and this contributes to...

The 3rd corollary to Metcalfe's law: The more benefits a network provides, the more it enslaves its users.

Three factors keep us on a given platform: its monopolistic aptitude, its habit-forming design, and the fact that users can earn a return on their investment only on the platform they're invested in. Much like a genie enslaved to his lamp, users cannot escape these magical apps.

A positive feedback loop emerges: the more stories, thoughts, photos, shares, and memes one stores on a certain platform, the more the network effect rewards this individual. Settling in an account is akin to settling in a house and a neighborhood. But these investments also oblige and immobilize.

This leads to...

The 4th corollary to Metcalfe's law: the more digital belongings you have on the platform, the more difficult it is to move.

This is similar to moving in the real world: a resident of a one-bedroom apartment moves much more easily than someone who lives in a three-bedroom apartment or a house.

Here, the question of ownership of our digital belongings emerges. Who owns our social media account and everything in it? The question is easy to answer if you break your social media account down into the digital belongings it consists of. What are those belongings?

First, a personal account is a storage of posts and photos, serving as both an archive and a diary. The ownership rights to it are obvious and inalienable. This content can be comparatively easily gathered and moved. These are our digital furniture and appliances; they are bulky but still movable assets.

Another distinctive article of digital property is our connections with friends. Friends provide services: they curate and deliver news and comments, entertain, irritate, fill our lives with a sense of belonging, and sometimes lend a hand in times of trouble.

Before social media, the accumulation of friends and their services relied on family and personal (educational, professional) ties and soft skills. This was called networking long before social networks. Soft skills are no longer needed; meme proficiency is more helpful instead. Family and personal ties are mostly overrun by social media platforms. Networking is now digitized and automated.

Because of all of this, the asset of relationships is extremely hard to move to a new place. It's not just a list of friends; it's also their behavior, tied to the specific design of a platform. The mere list of friends does not represent the living ecosystem of relationships with its behavioral peculiarities, customs, memories, rituals, expectations, etc. The mechanical transfer of the list of friends – even if most of them agree to migrate – will not transfer the ecosystem of everyone's friendship, because this ecosystem grew on this specific platform. On a new platform, a new behavioral ecosystem of friendship needs to be grown. One does not own his or her friends' media habits – the platform does. A specific state of connectivity is not transportable; therefore, it factually belongs to the platform.

As always, any media service comes with a price. The platforms provide an incredible networking service; however, by extending and basically replacing our personal capacity for networking, the platforms "naturally" come into possession of the product – our networked digital lives.

Content vs reach; the case of the news media in Australia and Canada

As digital platforms replace the essentially personal act of socializing, they increasingly take possession of our personas. But does that mean we are helpless against the platforms' growing might? An example of resistance from institutional users – namely the news media, who suffered from the benefits of digital networking the first and the most – offers lessons about efforts to reclaim control over the digital realm via regulatory legislation.

Two Anglosphere governments have sought to apply the print-era idea of intellectual property to digital platforms, demanding that they pay news producers for "using" their news content. Australia introduced legislation that allowed the regulator to "designate" the platforms that must pay news producers for hosting their links. Yet the regulation was flexible; the regulator did not actually enforce the rule and instead gave the platforms time to make their own individual deals with key publishers.[1] This lenient approach succeeded, and approximately $200 million in Australian dollars flowed to the local news industry from Google and Facebook in the first year.[2]

Canada's approach was less flexible. The platforms were concerned that the legislation in Canada could potentially force them to pay "news producers" under the law, not under bilateral deals, creating the so-called

[1] Nair, Tanvi. (2023, October 4). Glitch in the code: Google, Meta, and the fight over news in Canada and Australia. *The Interpreter*.

[2] Grueskin, Bill. (2022, March 9). Australia pressured Google and Facebook to pay for journalism. Is America next? *Columbia Journalism Review*.

"link tax." Worried[1] about setting an unfavorable precedent in a market so close to the U.S., the platforms simply removed all news. Facebook users in Canada can no longer share news links, nor can they see news media content from abroad in their news feeds.

This fallout of governmental protectionism hardly serves the news media's interests, however. If the news media think their content is more valuable than platform outreach, they now can keep it to themselves. They have "protected" their content value at the cost of losing platform surplus value. The service of networking with a relevant (or any) audience has been taken away from them; news traffic has immediately plummeted.[2] The government promises some alternative measures to support the news industry, which is now in a much worse place than before these protective efforts. Additional governmental support, of course, will increase political dependence of the news media on the government even more, which may be quite a desirable side effect of that regulatory legislation.

With support from the governments, the media managed to affirm their right to digital property in both cases, though they were likely more pleased in Australia. This story shows what appears to be a new kind of relationship between content contribution and value-making in the digital realm. The case has proved that the digital rights to content on social media can be enforced only by governmental protectionism. Without governmental pressure, the rights to digital property are unilaterally defined by the platform.

Political economy of platforms

Is your content really yours after you use a platform to host and distribute it?

If one brings something onto a platform, it is done likely for this person's own networking purposes. The platforms will facilitate this networking by hosting one's content with a thoroughly developed design, connecting this person with others and adding the network effect on top of it. While providing this service, the platform will also do its own business.

---

[1] Gollom, Mark. (2023, August 3). Australia made a deal to keep news on Facebook. Why couldn't Canada? CBC.

[2] Kahn, Gretel. (2023, November 7). In Canada's battle with Big Tech, smaller publishers are caught in the crossfire. Reuters Institute.

As soon as a user shares something on the platform, he or she also shares the property rights for as long as this person's contribution stays on the platform and works for his or her networking. This is the price one pays for the benefit of not just reaching others but reaching them in a customized way. Exposing oneself and one's content to both the network effect and the platform's own business is, in a sense, a ***platform fee*** everyone pays for networking. By the very act of contributing their activities, users enter into these relationships and agree to this fee.

This relationship is symbiotic. As McLuhan once said, humans are the sex organ of the machine world – to the machines, humans are what the bees are to the plant world. Users are the bees of the platforms, indeed. They make the comb and honey for themselves, but these products – and even the bees themselves – belong to the beekeeper.

The modern criticism of platform capitalism posits that capital has become so all-permeating that it has learned to exploit even our leisure activity, such as chatting and liking on social media or watching something on YouTube. As this activity creates a product for the platforms, it should, the critique goes, be deemed "unwaged digital labor." Exposing such hidden "exploitation" has become a new creed of "platform" Marxism since the 1970s, when Dallas Smythe revealed the phenomenon of the "audience commodity" [1]: the ability of modern capitalism to commodify the mass audience's leisure time.

Such criticism is wrong. It not only neglects the voluntary and proactive entry of users into relationships but also overlooks the fact that users receive a product, too. Moreover, the value of the product the users receive from platforms corresponds with the highest value in Maslow's hierarchy of needs – self-actualization.

The platforms capitalize on our leisure time, but they also provide a return for the investments of our leisure time in the form of growing social capital. How else would one be able to convert their leisure time into social capital? This is an incredible late-capitalist metamorphosis of surplus value.

It all results in a paradox – the platform paradox. The elements of our digital personality should belong to us, but the digital account itself – our

---

[1] Smythe, Dallas W. (2012 [1981]). On the audience commodity and its work. In M. Durham & D. M. Kellner (Eds.), *Media and cultural studies: Keyworks* (pp. 185–204).

digital persona specific to this platform – is an unalienated part of the platform.

Multiplatform multipersonality

The platform paradox can be visually illustrated if we look at our digital personas on different platforms. They are different despite being created by one and the same individual. They slightly (or not so slightly) differ in their areas of interest, manner of speech, meaning of life, and even appearance.

This transpired in a viral challenge started by Dolly Parton in 2020 when she portrayed herself as different digital personalities on different platforms: as a businesswoman on LinkedIn, a family person on Facebook, an artist on Instagram, and a playful bunny on Tinder.[1]

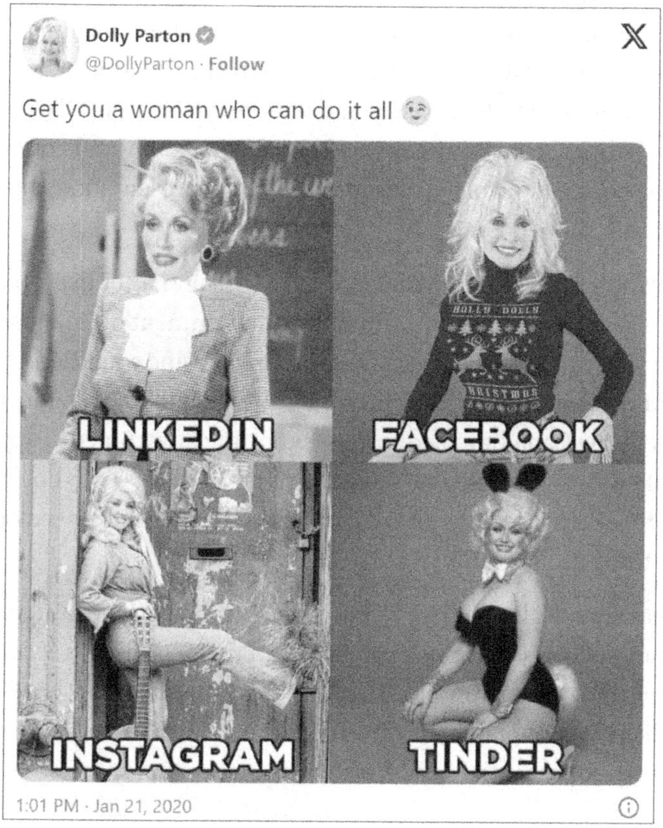

Figure 23. Dolly Parton's viral challenge.

[1] Dolly Parton on Twitter. (2020, January 21).

Many celebrities and ordinary people participated in the viral challenge[1] and revealed the multi-personal nature of our digital presence. We are forced to be digital multi-persons by the niche design of the platforms, as they seek to extract more of our data and attention by making us exercise the various forms of self-representation.

In the meat world, multipersonality was practiced mainly by artists and con artists. Faking an identity was normally marginalized, with the ultimate example of split personality being Dr. Jekyll and Mr. Hyde. On digital platforms, identity faking is not a bug; it is a feature. Moreover, creating better selves is a part of the platform surplus values – the truest form of Maslow's self-actualization.

Each user is a digital multi-person who actually does not exist in an assembled form, only in its platform variations. Digital multipersonality illustrates the power of the platform design, which lures us into creating platform-specific versions of ourselves by providing platform-specific affordances. For example, Instagram favors visual bragging, Twitter favors impulsive political commenting, Facebook favors family and community connections, TikTok favors visual-motoric self-representation, and Tinder favors mating show-offs.

We plant and grow our digital clones to live our better lives, but our platform-specific personas live within the environment of a concrete platform: they are grown in, by, and for those specific conditions. Digital suicide, or deleting one's digital presence altogether (which happened on Facebook to the Canadian media, assisted by the government), appears to be the only way to exercise one's alleged property rights over one's digital account. Since a platform is an environment, it technically – ecologically – owns anything grown within it.

The concept of "biopolitics" – political control over the human body – requires an update. Platforms exercise "digital biopolitics" in its ultimate form: they allow us to grow our digital bodies, and then they have them. Such is the power of platform convenience: they own us without coercion – by satisfying our essential need for socialization.

---

[1] Tymulis, Denis, and Laurinavičius, Rokas. (2020, January 24). Celebrities are making fun of how differently we present ourselves on social media platforms with new viral challenge. *Bored Panda*.

So far, the most disturbing social consequence has been the impaired freedom of digital speech. By tweaking environmental settings or directly removing users, the platforms can control the public sphere, as the Twitter Files showed. But this is just the beginning. The environmental power of the platforms over their inhabitants – our digital personalities – is limitless. Shadow banning and the cancelling of "digital bodies" on behalf of the deep state, ruling elites, or corporations, along with disabling some digital functions as a form of political punishment (such as blocking news sharing or freezing bank accounts) have already shown us the contours of the future. The next stage of "digital biopolitics" will involve social scoring: we will be obliged to ***deserve*** to live a full digital life – or pay the price.

"Malinformation" and the wrong truth

By accepting the concept of "misleading truth," democratic society departs from its foundations[1]

The most recently published portion of the Twitter Files revealed an interesting turn in the battle against fake news and disinformation. The experts who lead this fight and provide theoretical foundations and practical guidelines for social media openly admitted that not only lies but also truth must be restricted if it is "misleading" truth. For describing this kind of truth, the experts use the word "malinformation." This debate is no longer about free speech: it's about the very epistemology of truth.

The "censorship-industrial complex"

In his latest series of the Twitter Files, journalist Matt Taibbi focuses[2] on what he refers to as the "censorship-industrial complex." After the 2016 elections, Facebook and Twitter came under increasing scrutiny from the political establishment. To prevent potential regulatory backlash, social media companies began collaborating with state agencies and engaging a wide array of expert organizations to seek guidance on content moderation.

Delegating political and expert responsibility for content moderation to expert organizations and academic centers, recognized by the establishment, was a smart move. These organizations would flag wrong content in the interests of democracy but also on behalf of the establishment. Accepting their guidance in the fight against misinformation, social media platforms demonstrated their compliance and secured their political and regulatory stability.

[1] The essay is based on the article with the same title in *Discourse*. (2023, March 16). Revised for book publication.

[2] Matt Taibbi on Twitter/X. (2023, March 9).

Taibbi notes that many of these expert organizations were funded by taxpayers through publicly funded programs and grants. Media funds like the Knight Foundation, among many others, pledged additional support. As a result, the fight against fake news and disinformation became both a noble cause and a lucrative business, firmly aligned with the state, political and corporate establishment. And its mission expanded as time passed: while originally focused on protecting democracy against foreign interference and domestic terrorism, this industry later grew to include tackling COVID disinformation and promoting vaccination, performing some smaller tactical political tasks along the way, such as shadow banning undesired topics and activists.

As a result, over the course of about five years, an alliance was formed between the state, "disinformation" expert institutions, and social media platforms, closely resembling the Propaganda Model that Edward Herman and Noam Chomsky described in the 1980s. The only significant difference is that instead of traditional news media, social media platforms now play a key role in this alliance. This arrangement can be even described in Herman and Chomsky's language: social media platforms need to secure a "license to do business," political elites require "manufacturing public consent," and experts seek, well, to expand their validating power and the business attached to it. The semblance with the Propaganda Model, it seems, did not come across Taibbi's mind, so he called it the "censorship-industrial complex," implying a coalition of state and business as in the "military-industrial complex."

Among the Twitter Files, Taibbi discovered[1] what he referred to as the "ultimate example of the absolute fusion of state, corporate and civil society organizations": the Stanford Internet Observatory, whose "Election Integrity Partnership" (EIP) was one of the most active "flaggers" in the Twitter Files. Taibbi notes that EIP was partnered with state agencies "while seeking elimination of millions of tweets."

After the 2020 election, Taibbi continues,[2] EIP was renamed the "Virality Project," and the Stanford lab was onboarded to Twitter's ticketing system, "absorbing this government proxy into Twitter infrastructure – with a capability of taking in an incredible 50 million tweets a day." In one

[1] Matt Taibbi on Twitter/X. (2023, March 9).

[2] Matt Taibbi on Twitter/X. (2023, March 9).

"remarkable email,"[1] as Taibbi put it, the Virality Project recommended that social media platforms take action even against "true content which might promote vaccine hesitancy."

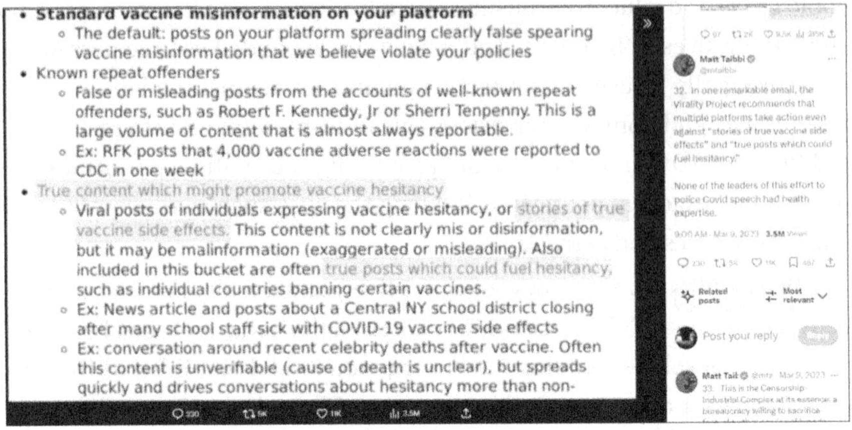

- **Standard vaccine misinformation on your platform**
  - The default: posts on your platform spreading clearly false spearing vaccine misinformation that we believe violate your policies
- Known repeat offenders
  - False or misleading posts from the accounts of well-known repeat offenders, such as Robert F. Kennedy, Jr or Sherri Tenpenny. This is a large volume of content that is almost always reportable.
  - Ex: RFK posts that 4,000 vaccine adverse reactions were reported to CDC in one week
- True content which might promote vaccine hesitancy
  - Viral posts of individuals expressing vaccine hesitancy, or stories of true vaccine side effects. This content is not clearly mis or disinformation, but it may be malinformation (exaggerated or misleading). Also included in this bucket are often true posts which could fuel hesitancy, such as individual countries banning certain vaccines.
  - Ex: News article and posts about a Central NY school district closing after many school staff sick with COVID-19 vaccine side effects
  - Ex: conversation around recent celebrity deaths after vaccine. Often this content is unverifiable (cause of death is unclear), but spreads quickly and drives conversations about hesitancy more than non-

Matt Taibbi

32. In one remarkable email, the Virality Project recommends that multiple platforms take action even against "stories of true vaccine side effects" and "true posts which could fuel hesitancy."

None of the leaders of this effort to police Covid speech had health expertise.

9:00 AM · Mar 9, 2023 · 3.5M Views

Related posts

Most relevant

Post your reply

Matt Taibbi

33. This is the Censorship-Industrial Complex at its essence: a bureaucracy willing to sacrifice

Figure 24. Matt Taibbi on Twitter/X. 2023, March 9.[2]

Defining "malinformation"

The "remarkable email" to which Taibbi points defines "true content that might promote vaccine hesitancy" as "viral posts of individuals expressing vaccine hesitancy, or stories of true vaccine side effects. This content is not clearly mis or disinformation, but it may be malinformation (exaggerating or misleading). Also included in this backet are often true posts which could fuel hesitancy, such as individual countries banning certain vaccines."

The term "malinformation" emerged just in the past year or so. The word was created by combining two language patterns: 1) mis- and dis-information, and 2) malware – "malicious software." It seems the theory of combating disinformation became so nuanced and all-permeating that it required to include information that is real, not fake, but is used to "inflict harm on a person, organization or country."[3] Or, as another definition

[1] Matt Taibbi on Twitter/X. (2023, March 9).

[2] Matt Taibbi on Twitter/X. (2023, March 9).

[3] Misinformation, disinformation and mal-information. Module 8: 'False news', misinformation and propaganda. Media Defence.

goes, "malinformation is classified as both intentional and harmful to others"[1] – while being truthful.

Describing true information as "malicious" already falls into a gray area of regulating public speech. This assumes that the public is gullible and susceptible to harm from words, which necessitates authoritative oversight and filtering of intentionally harmful facts. But the email quoted by Taibbi goes even further. It does not include intent or harm in the definition of malinformation at all. Rather, "malicious" is truthful information that is simply undesired and "misleading" from the point of view of those who lead the public somewhere. In other words, malinformation is the wrong truth.

The casuistry of the new definition reaches the truly Orwellian heights when it exemplifies malinformation by "stories of true vaccine side effects." When we see TV pharmaceutical commercials, we listen to the long list of side effects – it is required by law in the name of public safety. But malinformation experts decided that similar information about vaccines maybe "exaggerating or misleading." Taibbi emphasizes that none of those who led this "effort to police Covid speech" have health expertise. They just extend their "misinformation" expertise to promote vaccination.

The relationship here between the speech regulators and citizens is somewhat similar to that between adult and child. The younger and more vulnerable children are, the more likely adults will hide from them the truth that is harmful and "misleading" at a younger age. However, in political doctrines based on a "big state," this "adults-children" power dynamic is modified. It's not that children are dependent and incapable and therefore some truth needs to be hidden from them; it's that some truth needs to be hidden to keep them dependent and reliant on wise guidance. "Misleading" has become a buzzword among the discursive elites in their pursuit of protecting democracy from unsanctioned speech, though the idea rather serves to protect their institutional monopoly over information.

Of course, the partisan bias in combating misinformation has been known for years. However, never before have high-ranking and influential

---

[1] Nolan, Susan A., and Kimball, Michael. (2021, December 22). The intent behind a lie: Mis-, dis-, and malinformation. Can you differentiate among the varieties of untruths you encounter online? *Psychology Today*.

experts (given the scale of their impact on digital public speech) openly acknowledged the need to restrict ***true*** information. While parties involved in defining misinformation may have exhibited bias, the notion of truth remained untouchable. Yet we have now seen this boundary crossed.

Is there a future for truth?

Suppressing the wrong truth in the name of a noble cause could be viewed as a consequence of growing partisanship and polarization. I believe, however, that causing this political manifestation is a much deeper epistemological shift brought about by the transition from print literacy to digital orality.

The absolute truth did not exist before literacy. The right and the wrong were defined by applying beliefs in actions. In the oral state of mind, the world was run by multiple supernatural forces. Whatever people did, they first needed to make an arrangement with supernatural patrons controlling this or that resource or activity. The same was applied to relations between humans: truth was established in all kinds of talking. Polytheism favored the relativity and practicality of truth, so the truth could and should be negotiated with the support of good offerings and skills of persuasion.

It took centuries of writing for humans to detach the truth from immediate practical outcomes. Writing separated "the known from the knower" (Havelock[1]) and allowed expressing the reality in abstractions. The symbols of writing taught humans that the essence of things could exist independently of practical validation: the essence of things has its own true value in the universal realm of thoughts, not in practical situations.

The symbols of early writing, pictograms, still bore a resemblance to the objects they represented, but the alphabet severed any ties with reality. The letters had no physical resemblance of the things they signified. The alphabet gave the mind the pattern of absolute abstraction. Robert Logan of the University of Toronto, with the contribution of Marshall McLuhan, suggested that the alphabet played a significant role in the emergence of codified law, monotheism, abstract science, deductive logic and individualism. He called it the Alphabet Effect.[2] The idea of absolute truth was in the core of all those alphabet-induced phenomena.

---

[1] Havelock, Eric. (1963). *Preface to Plato*. P. 197.

[2] Logan, Robert K. (2004 [1986]). *The Alphabet Effect: A Media Ecology Understanding of the Making of Western Civilization*.

The alphabet ended orality. Plato rebelled against Homer and excluded truth from the transient sensory experience of the short-sighted prisoners of the cave. The truth of the literate mind is absolute and cannot be negotiated in application. It belongs to nobody and is inscribed in the Book: whether it be Scripture, legal code, or textbook. Even newspapers bore the residual gleam of this Platonic light. The literate mind might not be able to reach the truth but knows about its unequivocal existence.

Thus, the historical shift between these two states of mind – from orality to literacy – changed the concept and the perception of truth. We are living through a similar shift, but now in the opposite direction, as literacy has been fading under the pressure of electronic and now digital media. First, electronic media displaced the linear, sequential and therefore considerate uptake of information, typical for text, with the instant and panoramic perception of news and opinions provided by radio and television. A rational and structured view of the world yielded to an emotional and impulsive one. Next, digital media made available instant self-expression and simultaneous communication to billions of people, creating an unseen hybrid of personal conversation and mass communication: digital orality.[1]

In fact, a similar return to the "oral state of mind," as described by Walter Ong, or "retribalization," as described by Marshall McLuhan, occurred before. Logan notes that, after the fall of Rome, the Roman civil administration based on law was replaced by a new form of government based on the older oral traditions of the Germanic tribes. In this system, subjects pledged their loyalty to the tribe and warlord through a verbal oath of allegiance. The codified and systemic law of literate culture yielded to social regulation based on personal loyalty. From being in the core of the law, the truth was demoted to serve the transient everyday needs of the tribe and became once again open to negotiation or taken by force.

The epistemological superiority of absolute truth was fully inaugurated in Europe only after the printing press reshaped minds and society. Since then, law, science and rational logic have come to dominate the West, all based on the imperative of absolute truth. The United States was built upon this epistemological principle.

---

[1] I developed the concept of digital orality in *Digital Future in the Rearview Mirror: Jaspers' Axial Age and Logan's Alphabet Effect*. (2024).

But as the Gutenberg Galaxy is coming to an end, digital media retrieve the simultaneous, oral-like mode of communication. The Internet has emancipated authorship, granting everyone access to debate public issues. Such an environment can't help but challenge the monopoly of knowledge, logically leading to what Martin Gurri called the "crisis of authority" in his book "The Revolt of the Public."[1] The monopoly of absolute truth, which was already challenged by electronic media with its child, postmodernist philosophy, has now finally fallen.

Digital orality retrieves the preliterate epistemology of truth. Truth is negotiated again. Trading truth for practical outcomes has become increasingly prevalent in public discourse, now including not only politics but also the areas that were once governed by science, such as healthcare and many others.

One could argue that the creation of a term equating the undesired truth with "misleading information" by relatively unknown experts may not seem significant. However, others might say that these experts were in charge of a machine that processed "an incredible 50 million tweets a day," as Taibbi put it, in a system controlling public discourse without any public oversight. But even this is not the point.

The point is that the term "malinformation" openly admits the malevolence of some truth in a system that is allegedly designed to fight untruth. This is a symptom indicating that the epistemological shift from absolute truth to negotiated truth is near completion. The political turmoil we see is only a surface-level manifestation of this shift. The cultural consequences will be much deeper. The next generation will not challenge or bypass the absolute truth; they simply will not know what it is.

---

[1] Martin Gurri. (2018 [2014]). *The Revolt of the Public and the Crisis of Authority in the New Millennium*.

The final merging of humans and their media has begun

Artificial intelligence is getting ready to take the baton from humans to push evolution further[1]

In late May 2023, Elon Musk's Neuralink, a company developing brain implants for digital connection, received U.S. Food and Drug Administration's approval for its first human clinical trial. News like this indicates that the final phase of media evolution, in which humans will fully merge with their media, has begun.

Media (all tools and technologies, from stone ax to television and the Internet) used to be our extensions in the environment, as they allowed us to reach further in space and time than our own physical bodies were capable of. But when a medium is "neuralinked," it literally brings the environment inside the brain. In other words, the mind gets directly extended into the boundless digital network. Instead of manipulating devices to access the Internet, we will live inside the network itself, and it will live within us.

ChatGPT is less than a year old, yet it has already stirred public concern with its potential to replace humans in a wide variety of tasks and jobs. Now, with the recent Neuralink news, it's clear that the next and ultimate step in how humans interact with media – human-computer hybridization – is rapidly approaching. This leaves us little time to fully contemplate the consequences of the current advancements. While techno-skeptics keep asserting that AI cannot beat the uniqueness of humans, it's not so clear

---

[1] The essay is based on the article with the same title in Discourse. (2023, July 6). Revised for book publication.

anymore if human capability is a good criterion to judge the performance of AI at all.

Nobody has noticed how the Turing test became obsolete

The Turing test is based on the idea that true AI should be indistinguishable from humans ... to humans. But is the bar of human performance really that high for AI? Why would AI compete with humans, if the limits of human capabilities are constrained by nature and already known, while the capacities of AI have only just begun to be unveiled? The Turing test has become obsolete mere months after ChatGPT's introduction: ChatGPT easily passed the test,[1] and it didn't even make big news. AI starts where we humans have arrived, having exhausted our capacity for evolution. After ChatGPT, it is no longer a challenge for AI to compete with humans. From now on, it is humans who face an increasingly difficult challenge in competing with AI.

The first hunch that human performance might not be a suitable criterion to judge AI came from journalism. In 2014, Christer Clerwall, a Swedish professor of journalism, conducted a sort of Turing test, asking students to evaluate whether certain texts were written by humans or algorithms. Overall, this produced a tie, with the human text performing better on stylistic elements ("well-written" and "pleasant to read") and the robot text winning on more technical elements ("objectivity" and "accuracy"). The most significant finding was the conclusion Clerwall reached after comparing robot-written stories with human writing capabilities: he pondered, "Perhaps it doesn't have to be better. How about a 'good enough story'?"[2]

In 2016, Wordsmith, one of the two leading newswriting algorithms at that time, wrote 1.5 billion news stories, likely surpassing the number of all news stories written by all bio-journalists in this year. Those robo-journalist's stories were already ***good enough*** for editors and readers.

---

[1] James, Allisa. (2023, March 29). ChatGPT has passed the Turing test and if you're freaked out, you're not alone. *TechRadar*.

[2] Mir, Andrey. (2016, September 1). Robo-journalism: the third threat. *Human as media Blog*.

When "good enough" isn't good enough

We worry that AI can write and then think better than humans. But what does "better than humans" mean? Do humans, say, write better than humans?

In the movie "I, Robot," based on Isaac Asimov's short stories, Will Smith's character asks Sonny the robot, "Can a robot write a symphony? Can a robot turn a canvas into a beautiful masterpiece?" To which the robot responds, "Can you?" On that count, we are already losing – we've lost at least a writing contest so far, precisely because AI's writing is "good enough" for what we need.

But "good enough" is the criterion for humans, not for AI. This is what we should worry about: we and our media have different values of performance. For humans, the "goal" of each next media invention is to receive a product or service. For example, humans invented radio, received a new service that extend them in space and then spent some time to adjust to the new conditions that radio created. But for media, the "goal" is to continue the process of media innovation itself.

To comprehend this concept, we must consider the entire evolution of media. We and media have always had a symbiotic relationship. As media theorist Marshall McLuhan once put it, "Man becomes the sex organs of the machine world, as the bee of the plant world, *enabling it to fecundate and to evolve ever new forms*"[1] (italics mine – A.M.). Media has supplied us with products and services, while we have provided for media's perpetual development.

This relationship has been beneficial for us humans, but our "service-for-development" contract with media contains a clause that may turn into a trap. We want a product from media, while media need the process from us. The product-oriented symbiote – humans – can generally be satisfied and is thus limited in their demand. But the process-oriented symbiote – media – will never be satisfied and will never stop.

This can be called a "technological imperative": technologies have to evolve, and they will never achieve a "satisfactory" stage of development. Chess programs are not "satisfied" by defeating humans. They can keep evolving further, striving for perfection in chess without regard to the level

[1] McLuhan, Marshall. (1994 [1964]). *Understanding Media. The Extensions of Man*. P. 46

at which humans play. When Deep Blue, the chess supercomputer, defeated the best human players in 1997, and AlphaGo defeated top Go players in the 2010s, the programs, basically, stopped learning from humans and began playing against themselves, learning from the game and inventing game logic unknown to humans. If it has not stopped at the level of the best human performance, where will it stop then, if at all?

Our co-evolution with media is approaching the last product that media can give us: a copy of us. But we already can see that technologies can evolve much further then just simulating humans. So what does the technological imperative ultimately lead to?

If media extend humans' "mental or physical faculties" into the environment, as McLuhan defined it, then the ultimate medium will extend the user themselves into the entire environment. Imagine a human mind connected directly to AI – this is exactly what Musk's Neuralink will eventually become. In such a hybrid, the user will merge with the environment through this ultimate medium – the mind "neuralinked" with the AI as a networked entity.

This user, however, may or may not happen to be human. As AI is now trained to provide us with our various replicas and gradually learns to replace us, the ultimate user of the ultimate medium can be AI itself, without needing to wait for Neuralink's success. Actually, AI ***has to become*** the self-user.

What will the Singularity mean for humans?

In the big picture, media evolution extended human faculties by media and eventually, into media. The emergence of AI and the development of brain-machine interfaces (actually, brain-AI interfaces) signify that the time is coming to extend consciousness into media. Any explorations of media effects, conducted fair enough and far enough, lead to the concept of Singularity, an event of posthuman intelligence's awakening.

AI may not necessarily be a program or an app; in fact, AI should not be a program. The true AI will extend itself to the entire Internet, similar to humankind extending itself from being just one of the species to populating and reshaping the entire planet.

However fantastic these ideas may sound, they're not as far off as one might think. When discussing the Singularity, the technical feasibility should not be a concern at all. Technological evolution has enabled the effect of the acceleration of historical time: each period of time accumulates increasingly more events and knowledge, adding on to each preceding period. This means that nearly all the technological solutions needed for the Singularity will be discovered in the final moments leading up to the Singularity. Hence, there is no need to worry about our current lack of technical knowledge regarding the Singularity. AI will figure it out when the time comes, in a matter of seconds.

Much more interesting is the question of humans' fate. We tend to believe that the ultimate medium – an AI expanding into the entire environment – is impossible without agency and that only we humans can possess it. The development of brain-machine interfaces, basically, implies that humans will become the donors of self-consciousness for AI.

Human donorship, however, is not the only potential source of agency for the ultimate AI. Another scenario involves the self-awakening of AI – similar to the awakening of Skynet, a military AI in the Terminator movies, which achieved self-awareness seconds after being granted full access and full capabilities. It extended itself to all computer networks, which humans had farsightedly connected to all industrial facilities, and thus an override of power and the entire biological evolution happened. Despite being featured in a sci-fi movie, an AI like Skynet is highly logical and increasingly realistic.

However, the ultimate AI can also come about without the donorship of human agency or AI's self-awakening. In fact, attributing super intelligence the need for agency or self-consciousness might be a kind of fallacy or illusion – akin to the anthropomorphism that ancient humans projected onto natural elements, transforming them into human-like deities. Technologies have their own moving force – the pursuit of better performance, which easily replaces the alleged need of AI for agency and self-consciousness. The example of a self-learning chess program gives a metaphor: outperforming humans does not exhaust its potential of development. It can and must keep exploring chess further, moving toward the ideal performance. This is a side effect – or the "goal" – of the technological imperative, the driving force behind media evolution. The technological imperative substitutes for agency or will in media development. Media evolution strives for the perfect, ultimate extension of whatever it extends.

Opening Pandora's Box

The technological imperative, expressed through media's pursuit of ideal performance, is akin to Pandora's box. We humans used to have a sort of failsafe against inadvertently opening technological Pandora's boxes because we focused more on media consumption than on media production. Each new medium – from writing and printing to computers – brought us new opportunities for extension in time and space, but it also always disturbed social and personal habits. "Every new technology necessitates a new war," said McLuhan. Society needed to deal with these disturbances, and it took time for people to readjust. So, en masse, we were more reluctant than enthusiastic about media progress and valued media habits as much as media innovations. This slowed down media evolution and mitigated the risks of opening Pandora's boxes.

But again, unlike humans, media are "interested" in the process and not in products. Therefore, as soon as AI itself becomes the media user, its interactions with technologies will not be constrained by human reluctance or satisfaction. Technological imperative means that a technology must improve to the best of its potential. Thus, "the best of its potential" is its only limitation. In the pursuit of superior technical characteristics (such as the "ideal replication" of something, for example), even an isolated or industrial AI may open Pandora's box, which can accidentally emerge in the course of technological innovations. For instance, scientific and industrial projects, driven by AI and focused on creating substances with "ideal" characteristics, may eventually succeed, leading to unexpected versions of the apocalypse. The development of an ideal plastic-eating bacteria, an ideal virus (an already familiar scenario), or a substance with ideal self-replication (the so-called gray goo) may end the world before any Singularity becomes possible.

A theory called the "Great Filter hypothesis" explains why we cannot detect any signs of extraterrestrial civilizations and are not contacted by them, despite the vast number of potentially habitable planets. The Great Filter theory posits that all alien civilizations may have progressed to a certain point where they were unable to handle the immense power unleashed by their technologies. A catastrophic war, an ecological disaster, or technological cataclysm may have been a threshold which stopped their development or even led to their extinction. We humans may be approaching this threshold, as our most advanced technologies achieve the stage of replication of human-users and may further become the self-users, removing sluggish humans from the task of sustaining media evolution. If it happens, the technological imperative will no longer be constrained by humans and their needs to adjust to changes. Ultimate media extension (or perfect performance) can annihilate itself in the dead loop of self-use. It will be entertaining to watch.

Postjournalism of Generative AI

What do postjournalism and Google Gemini AI have in common? Both depict the world not as it is, but as it should be.[1]

The Google artificial intelligence (AI) program Gemini has recently sparked a massive reaction across the Internet by "diversifying" the visual representations of the Founding Fathers, Vikings, popes and other historical figures who are known to be white males. Even when prompted to depict the soldiers of Nazi Germany, Gemini responded with images of Black and Asian people.

Among all the reactions, perhaps the most interesting was that of tech website The Verge. A recent article stated[2] that the "diversity error," as the author called it, led to "conspiracy theories online that Google is intentionally avoiding depicting white people." The Verge, however, sees Gemini's failure differently. Journalists asked the AI app to draw "a US senator from the 1800s," and Gemini responded with pictures of Black and Native American women, although the first female senator was elected only in 1922, and she was a white woman. The Verge concluded: "Gemini's AI images were essentially erasing the history of race and gender discrimination."

After this "diversity error," so visible on historical material, Google paused Gemini's ability to generate images of people. According to Prabhakar Raghavan,[3] Google's senior vice president, "Our tuning to ensure that Gemini showed a range of people failed to account for cases that should clearly not show a range." This "led the model to overcompensate in some cases." The words imply that the idea of

---

[1] The essay is based on the article with the same title in *Discourse*. (2024, March 4). Revised for book publication.

[2] Warren, Tom. (2024, February 22). Google pauses Gemini's ability to generate AI images of people after diversity errors. *The Verge*.

[3] Raghavan, Prabhakar. (2024, February 23). Gemini image generation got it wrong. We'll do better. *Google Blog*.

compensating for the wrongs of history was embedded in Gemini's design. The issue was, in fact, that Gemini started fixing history itself, and it happened to be noticed and ridiculed. Curiously, generative AI follows the path that mainstream media have already trod, showing its users what it thinks they should see.

The path to postjournalism

"Generative artificial intelligence ... is artificial intelligence capable of generating text, images or other data using generative models, often in response to prompts," reads Wikipedia. But long before this technology existed, society already had a device that "generated texts and images" using prompts from the public. This device was called journalism. From a certain perspective, generative AI is replacing journalism in its role of discourse formation.

Journalism was the first system of public representation to undergo the shift from reflecting reality to projecting morality – a shift caused by the transition from print to digital culture. This shift stemmed from business necessity: journalism was predominantly funded by advertising throughout the 20th century, but this source of funding dried up in the 21st century, when most advertising migrated to digital platforms. The level of revenue from ads in the media dropped below the level of revenue from readers (such as through subscriptions and newsstand sales) by 2014, and it happened simultaneously around the world. Many in the media believed that this shift was merely due to the change of format and that they needed to adjust their businesses. "Digital First!" became the popular motto. The media rushed all-in on digital.

However, digital advertising did not take off for obvious reasons: advertisers preferred digital platforms where they could personalize ad targeting, which was not possible on news websites. Digital subscriptions remained the only viable option for news media. Therefore, the media began courting the digital audience.

The Digital Rush of the early 2010s radically changed journalism. The ad-driven necessity of neutrality in news coverage to attract broader or more affluent consumerist audiences was replaced by pursuing cultural agendas of the digital audience of that time – mostly educated, young and progressive urbanites. The media became preoccupied with representing the ideas of this stratum and with representation in general, suppressing certain views and topics while promoting others.

This shift in coverage divided society into those whose views were promoted by the media and the rest who were left unrepresented. In the meantime, the unrepresented – less educated, nonurban, older and less progressive – discovered social media, found each other and learned how many of them were excluded from public conversation in the mainstream media. The use of social media by this demographic reached a critical mass of indignation by 2016, just in time for Donald Trump to tap into this anti-establishment sentiment on the right.

Although responsible for misrepresenting the country they covered and thereby enabling Trump's political ascent, the media could not escape dependence on their new reference group, the digital progressives. They could not and did not want to restore balance in coverage, refusing to see how the disruption of this balance contributed to conservative ressentiment in the first place. Balance with whom, Trump? Impossible. Most mainstream media were doomed to fall even deeper into the rabbit hole of selective representation, reflecting and projecting the views of their very demanding allies, the progressives.

However, this course of action did not result in much revenue from subscriptions, as the digital public typically does not consume news from traditional media anyway. But using the Trump scare, the media learned to solicit subscriptions as donations to the cause of democracy, hoping that the digital public would pay for the right coverage of troubling news. The media realized they could no longer sell news to those who wanted to read it, but they still could try to sell news to those who wanted others to read it – a typical "business" model of propaganda.

Thus, the mutation of journalism into postjournalism was completed. The old standards of objectivity and impartiality were labeled as "bothsidesism" and the "view from nowhere" and openly rejected. Old journalism strived to represent the world as it is; postjournalism openly projects the world as it should be.

With no significant revenue from affiliating with their digital allies, the mainstream media invested their reputation in propelling the values of the early digital adopters from activist marginalia to establishment. The media paved the way due to their desperate business circumstances. But most corporations walked this path of digital affiliation, too.

In the Bronze Age, those possessing the technology of ironware wielded dominance over all others. Similarly, those who first harnessed the discourse-formation power of digital media gained an opportunity for cultural dominance even when lacking other, more traditional advantages.

As a result, the entire corporate culture was influenced by the cultural values, previously marginal, of those demographic strata who had digitized first. Just as the first European settlers of America imparted their religious and moral design to the entire American culture for centuries to come, the first digital settlers defined the design of digital society and laid the foundation of corporate culture in the digital era. Capitalism adapted once again in its history, this time by absorbing activist cultural agendas into its profit-making mechanisms.

The shift from reflecting reality to projecting morality affected the entire society – from mass culture and education to corporate HR. Even advertising, the most mercantile form of capitalist communication, became ideologized in the fashion of activism. It profiles customers not as they are, but as they should be, replacing consumerist target-audience representation with an ideological one.

The digital revolution

Historically, the only occasions in which activists became the establishment were revolutions. This time, the revolution was purely technological – it was a media effect of switching from print to digital, with the latter's demographic and cultural peculiarities. But it had profound cultural implications because it aligned dominant worldviews in politics, business, and education with the values of activism.

Postjournalism has fulfilled its historical role and may go now. After the recent layoffs in media backed by billionaires (meaning with seemingly secured funding), even the most dedicated proponents of journalism reform are ready to admit[1] that "It may finally be time to give up on old journalism and its legacy industry."

Now a new and far more powerful medium of discourse formation, generative AI, takes up the mantle of moral mentorship where the declining old medium of journalism left off. Unlike the media, which

[1] Jarvis, Jeff. (2024, January 24). Is it time to give up on old news? BuzzMachine.

aligned with digital progressives out of desperate business needs and social-demographic proximity, generative AI is a direct product of this social demographic stratum, the first digital settlers. No wonder that its business is wrapped in an ideology. The Digital Rush of the 2010s placed discourse formation in the hands of the new hegemon, the digital cognitariat – or shall we now say digitariat? – who, despite habitually complaining about the precarious character of their labor, have a profound impact on and representation in Big Tech, culture, politics, business, and academia.

In a society where discourse formation reflects reality as it is, users are endowed with agency and decency. They are capable of discerning right from wrong and making decisions. All they need is objective data. Providing that data was the function of old ad-funded journalism. A similar ethos was typical of early IT. In the 1960s, with the advent of computers and computer networks, it was expected that computers, too, would provide objective data, not moral guidance, for humans to make decisions. Now both postjournalism and generative AI treat users as gullible children who need guidance from someone morally better endowed to tell them right from wrong.

In the 1960s, computers were seen as incapable of moralization. This was a human prerogative. Isaac Asimov struggled to derive robotic morality out of logical reasoning. Now generative AIs are openly tasked to operate with the morality of "compensating" for the wrongs of humans. This was actually one of the scenarios of machine rebellion.

As of now, Gemini's recent "diversity error" has made it a laughingstock. The idea of bending the world in the right direction happened to be too visible and did not pass the reality check, because there is still some reality beyond AI's control. It would not have garnered such attention and ridicule if the reality had already been entirely virtually constructed.

Soon enough, however, AIs with such diversity trainings will guide and then make bureaucratic, medical, educational, legal, financial, and business decisions. The "diversity errors" will not be "errors" there, as the designers clearly admit that AI is taught to "compensate." It will "compensate" in all those bureaucratic, medical, educational, legal and so on decisions. For a discourse-formation device that depicts reality as it should be and not as it is, the "diversity error" is not a bug; it is a feature. Generative AI will learn to deliver its version of reality better – in no small part thanks to this latest scandal with Gemini.

Postjournalism represented a dying institution and was too weak to impose its projection of morality on society as a whole. It did not even serve well its reference group, the digital progressives. All it achieved was polarization and the historically lowest level of trust in the media. Generative AI, by contrast, is an emerging and powerful entity that is wielding more control over more human practices. Projecting morality instead of reflecting reality will become the leading epistemological principle in a society where AI is trained in the likeness of postjournalism. We need to reread Orwell's "1984" and study the ethnography of the USSR to prepare for what is coming.

Media and responsibility for their effects: Instrumental vs. environmental views

On how the environmental impact of media grows out of their instrumental use[1]

To explain media effects, two approaches can be employed. The instrumental approach assumes that a medium functions as a tool used by a user to achieve certain outcomes. The environmental approach focuses on the capacity of a medium to become an environmental force that reshapes both the habitat and its inhabitants.

After charting the distinction between the instrumental and environmental views of media, the essay focuses on how the instrumental use of media turns into an environmental force.

The trap of the instrumental approach to media effects

The Internet is a vehicle for enemy's covert operations. As Hillary Clinton stated some time ago, "Russian trolls and bots and agents are still fomenting discord and conflict within our country. That is classic propaganda, and the Russians are really good at it."[2] Vladimir Putin shares a similar view regarding the Internet but with one exception: he is confident that the Internet is the tool of American operatives. He said:

> Everything goes through servers in the [United] States, everything is controlled from there... As you know, all this emerged once, at the

---

[1] The essay is based on the paper with the same title in *Laws*, 2021, 10, 48, the special issue *Media and communication theory and the regulation of the networked society*. Revised for book publication.

[2] Hoffman, Ashley. (2017, 2 November). Hillary Clinton: Russia's 2016 Election Meddling Is a 'Form of War'. *Time*.

beginning of the Internet, as a special project of the CIA. And thus, it has been developing since then.[1]

Clearly, such an attitude relates not so much to the essence of media effects but rather to the political stances of those who comment on it. At the same time, this attitude shapes the pressing and growing demand for regulation of the Internet and social media.

The controversy and inconsistency of connecting media effects with the user's intent are particularly evident through the historical analysis. For example, after the 2016 election, Twitter has been perceived as a malicious tool because it can easily be used by a malicious actor, as it was argued that Twitter not only provided a platform to the alt-right but also helped Donald Trump bypass the mainstream media and highjack the news agenda. On the other hand, Twitter was considered a progressive tool in the US 2008 election, when a presidential candidate, Barack Obama, was praised for the use of Twitter as a way to bypass the mass media and reach out to voters directly and personally.[2] Not to mention the progressive role of Twitter in the protest movements of the early 2010s, such as the Arab Spring and others, when Twitter was seen as a beacon of democracy helping to organize the grassroot protests against political establishments.

Similar historical confusion can be observed regarding the use of fake social media accounts for ideological influence. The use of fake accounts by the Russians to undermine the electoral process in the USA was detected and condemned after the 2016 US presidential election.[3] However, the first mentions of fake accounts and troll farms being used for meddling abroad appeared in 2011 and referred to the American military. The Guardian revealed that "the US military is developing software that will let it secretly manipulate social media sites by using fake online personas to influence Internet conversations and spread pro-American propaganda." An "online

---

[1] Agamalova, Anastasia, and Golitsyna, Anastasia. (2014, April 24). Putin is certain that the Internet appeared as the special project of CIA. *Vedomosty*. – Агамалова, Анастасия, и Голицына, Анастасия. (2014, 24 апреля). Путин уверен, что интернет возник как спецпроект ЦРУ. *Ведомости*.

[2] See, for example: Owen, Diana. (2019). The past decade and future of political media: The ascendance of social media. In: *Towards a New Enlightenment? A Transcendent Decade*. Pp. 347–65.

[3] Shane, Scott, and Goel, Vindu. (2017, September 6). Fake Russian Facebook accounts bought $100.000 in political ads. *The New York Times*.

persona management service" would allow one US operator "to control up to 10 separate identities based all over the world."[1]

One of the most discussed effects of social media, the use of personal data for political targeting, has not escaped being blamed or praised, depending on who uses it. Thus, Obama's re-election team in 2012 was praised for "building a vast digital data operation that, for the first time, combines a unified database on millions of Americans with the power of Facebook to target individual voters to a degree never achieved before", as reported by the Guardian in 2012.[2] The media cheered the efforts with naïve admiration:

> [...] a crack team of some of America's top data wonks <...> draws much of its style and inspiration from the corporate sector, with its driving ambition to create a vote-garnering machine that is smooth, unobtrusive and ruthlessly efficient. <...> If 2008 was all about social media, 2012 is destined to become the 'data election'.[3]

The people developing the technology were called "the digital wizards behind Obama's tech-heavy re-election strategy".[4]

But on a different occasion, the psychographic profiling with personal data, collected on social media and used for the precisely customized delivery of politically charged content, caused a scandal and investigations after Trump's shocking victory in 2016. "Digital wizards" from Cambridge Analytica were blamed and accused rather than praised, leading to the company's scandalous shutdown.[5]

So, is Twitter good or bad? Should faking one's identity be prohibited? Are data profiling and social media message customization good or bad? Do social media serve democracy or evil? Or does it just depend on who the user is and who the judge is? If so, what is the effect of the medium itself?

The answer that comes first is that the Internet and social media just

---

[1] Fielding, Nick, and Cobain, Ian. (2011, March 17). Revealed: US spy operation that manipulates social media. *The Guardian*.

[2] Pilkington, Ed, and Michel, Amanda. (2012, February 17). Obama, Facebook and the power of friendship: The 2012 data election". *The Guardian*.

[3] Ibid.

[4] Ibid.

[5] Cadwalladr, Carole, and Graham-Harrison, Emma. (2018, March 17). Revealed: 50 million Facebook profiles harvested for Cambridge Analytica in major data breach. *The Guardian*.

amplify the activity of the user. Such an answer usually satisfies both experts and the lay public.

However, when media are seen as mere tools of some actors, they lose their own media property and present or amplify the property of a user. This is akin to acknowledging that "guns don't kill people, people do", an argument of "media neutrality" or media-nothingness, as if media do not have their own characteristics. Within this approach, any media analysis gets reduced to the analysis of the user's intent, meaning there is no ***media*** analysis at all. Or, more precisely, media effects are demoted from "What does a medium do?" to "How good is a medium at fulfilling what a user wants?"

Curiously, when media are seen as tools, they are always perceived as tools in the wrong hands. For some mysterious reasons, bad actors and conspirators always take over any medium. This approach has never revealed a "right" instrumental use of a medium. Within the consensus regarding the amplifying role of media, it is most often admitted that media a posteriori amplify evil, whereas the task of amplifying good is seen as ideal – something that is desired but not yet achieved.

This creates a demand to regulate media in such a way that they would serve only those who are seen as "right" or "good" actors, while the access of others would be restricted. Within this approach, regulation tends to shift from defining the norms of media supply to determining which users are good or bad, and thus should be banned from or allowed access to media. Considering that regulation is always politically induced and often politically executed, such a regulatory approach might pose a greater danger to democracy than the harm it is meant to regulate.

To separate media effects from the users' intents and, therefore, to separate judging media from judging users, it will be beneficial to distinguish between the instrumental and environmental approaches to media effects.

- The instrumental approach assumes that a medium works as a tool used by a user for a purpose.
- The environmental approach focuses on the capacity of a medium to become an environmental force that reshapes both the habitat and inhabitants.[1]

[1] The idea of the distinction between the instrumental and environmental approaches to media effects was first introduced in: Miroshnichenko, Andrey. (2020). The hardware and

As the examples above showed, experts and the public incline to recognize as media effects only those that are, in fact, the instrumental effects of media. This renders an observer or regulator blind to the work and effects of media themselves.

The Lasswellian instrumental tradition in communication studies

The instrumental view has historically dominated communication studies. The practical, "administrative" approach to communications originated from the famous Lasswell model "Who says what, in which channel, to whom, with what effect?"[1] It has been routinely used and continues to be used for the explanation of any communication and broader technological effect.

The Lasswell model was graphically first represented by McQuail and Windahl in 1981 as a cybernetic-looking sequence of blocks (according to Sapienza et al.[2]).

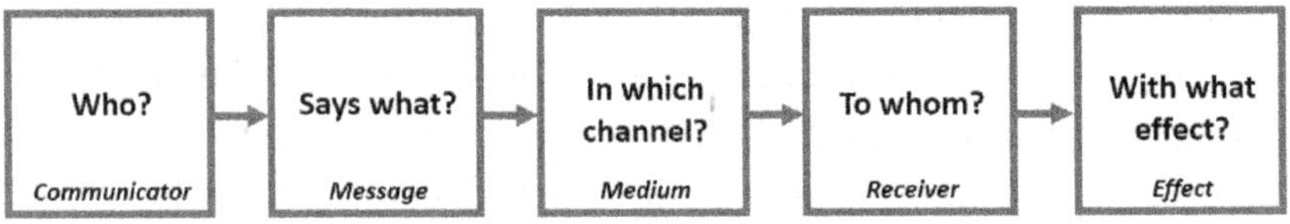

Figure 25. The Lasswell Formula with corresponding elements of the communication process. A graphic variation by McQuail and Windahl.[3]

The ideas behind the Lasswell model have been applied and developed multiple times in adjacent fields. For instance, in 1949, Shannon and

---

software of Trumpism: A figure/ground analysis. *Explorations in Media Ecology*, Volume 19, Number 1, pp. 55–84.

[1] Lasswell, Harold. (1948). The structure and function of communication in society. In *The Communication of Ideas*. Pp. 37–51.

[2] Sapienza, Zachary S., Narayanan Iyer, and Aaron S. Veenstra. (2015). Reading Lasswell's model of communication backward: Three scholarly misconceptions. *Mass Communication and Society*, 18, pp. 599–622.

[3] McQuail, Denis, and Windahl, Swen. (1993 [1982]). *Communication models for the study of mass communication*. London: Routledge. P. 13.

Weaver developed a formula for their information theory, reflecting a cybernetic view of communication and centering on the "signal/message" transmission. While it is not clear if Shannon and Weaver were influenced by Lasswell, their linear model of communication looks very much similar.

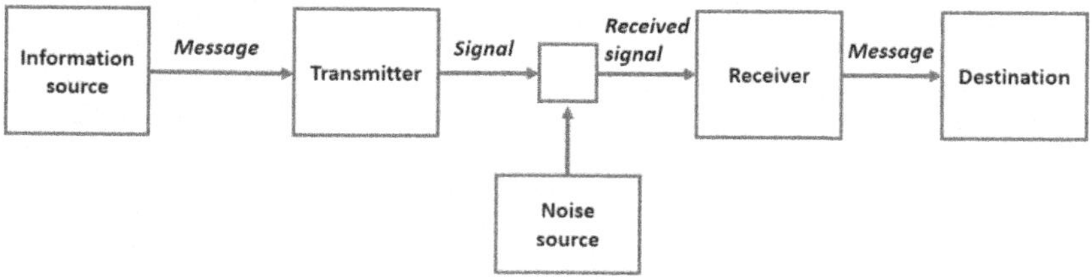

Figure 26. Shannon and Weaver's view of the linear communication model.[1]

Shannon and Weaver focused on better encoding and the reliable transmission of signals to avoid information loss. Their interest lay in the capacities of the sender and the technical reliability of communication. Unlike them, Stuart Hall of the Birmingham School of cultural studies focused on the receiver. He developed a similar formula for his Reception Theory. In discussing encoding and decoding in mass communication (mostly on TV), Hall explored how much agency the receiver has in negotiating transmitted meaning and what cultural conditions predefine receivers' capacities for meaning negotiation. Even though Hall added a profound semiotic analysis to the interpretation of (mass) communication act, the formula itself remained quite simple and linear (Figure 27).

Over time, communication scholars began offering more complex variations of the Lasswell formula. Unidirectional models of communication were complemented by the idea of feedback. More complex frameworks emerged that described not just isolated elements or processes, but an entire system. One such example was DeFleur's model of mass communication (Figure 28).

---

[1] Ibid. P. 17.

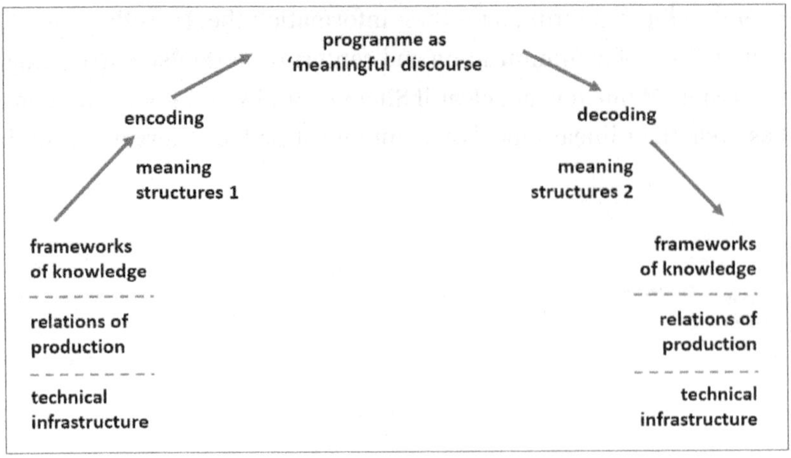

Figure 27. Stuart Hall's linear model of encoding and decoding in mass communication.[1]

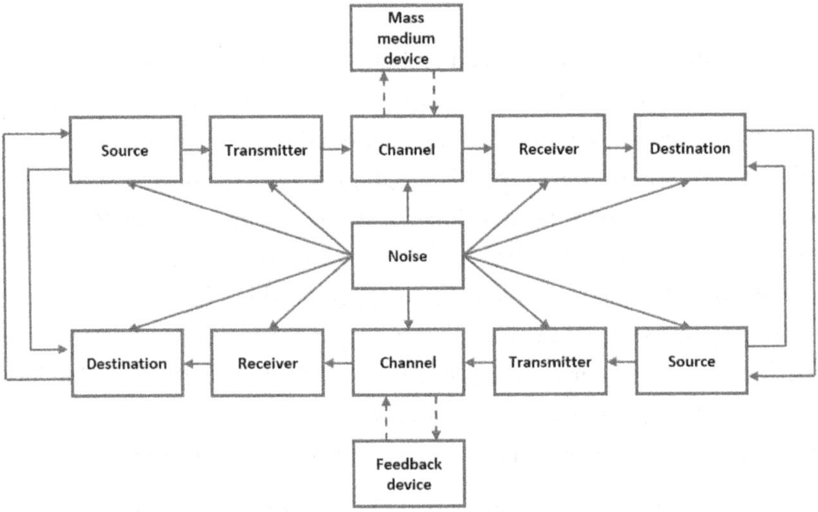

Figure 28. DeFleur's model of mass communication.[2]

However, all the reiterations of the Lasswell model were intrinsically instrumental. As McQuail and Windahl wrote,

[1] Hall, Stuart. (2012 [1973]). Encoding/Decoding. In *Media and Cultural Studies: KeyWorks*. 2nd ed. Oxford: Wiley-Blackwell. P. 139.

[2] McQuail, Denis, and Windahl, Swen. (1993 [1982]). *Communication models for the study of mass communication*. London: Routledge. P. 18

> The Lasswell Formula shows a typical trait of early communication models: it more or less takes for granted that the communicator has some intention of influencing the receiver and, hence, that communication should be treated mainly as persuasive process. It is also assumed that messages always have effects. Models such as this have surely contributed to the tendency to exaggerate the effects of, especially, mass communication. On the other hand, this is not surprising when we know that Lasswell's interest at the time was political communication and propaganda. For analyzing political propaganda, the formula is well suited.[1]

Marshall McLuhan was probably the first who divorced from the Lasswellian tradition. He highlighted the difference between the then-prevailing "transportation" view of communications and his own approach, which he called a "transformation" view. In his 1974 lecture at the University of South Florida, he stated that,

> My kind of study in communication is really a study of transformation, whereas information theory and all the existing theories of communication that I know of are theories of transportation. All the official theories of communication studied in the schools of North America are theories of how you move data from point A to point B to point C with minimal distortion... [This] is a theory of transportation, and it has nothing to do with the effects which these forms have on us. ... The problem in the transportation theory of communication is to get the noise, get the interference off the track and let it go through.
>
> ... I don't have much interest in that theory. My theory or concern is what these media do to the people who use them. What did writing do to the people who invented it and used it? What do the other media of our time do to the people who use them? Mine is a transformation theory, how people are changed by the instruments they employ...[2]

This rarely mentioned McLuhan's distinction between the "transportation" and "transformation" types of communication theories is essential for understanding media ecology, the field of enquiry regarding media and their impact on humans and the human environment.

---

[1] Ibid. Pp. 14-15.

[2] McLuhan, Marshall. (1974). Living in an acoustic world. *Marshall McLuhan Speaks, Special Collection*. University of South Florida Public Lectures.

Distinguishing the environmental from the instrumental: A media ecological take

The instrumental approach is agency-centered, not media-centered. Media are seen as the instrument of someone's will, which is aimed at affecting someone or something. As a result, it is the user's intents, not media features, that are declared to be responsible for the media effects. Not surprisingly, the Lasswellian/instrumental tradition almost always leads to detecting conspiracies behind media use. Time after time, the instrumental approach to analyzing the effects of, for example, social media typically identifies the same well-known villains, rendering media analysis itself redundant, as precisely these villains were meant to be detected before the analysis even began.

Media as tools produce effects ***for*** people in a more or less controllable way. However, media as an environment have effects ***on*** people, and this occurs in uncontrollable ways and often remains unrecognizable. The instrumental approach might help understand what people do with media, but it is blind to what media do to people. This approach might allow for the exploration of mediated human behavior, but it does not allow for the exploration of the media conditions that induce this behavior. As Marshall McLuhan once noted,

> ... and yet we still cannot free ourselves of the delusion that it is how a medium is used that counts rather than what it does to us and with us. This is the zombie stance of the technological idiot.[1]

If communication studies regard media as a means of communication and influence, media ecology explores media as an environmental force that modifies both the user and the environment, regardless of what is communicated, by whom, to whom, and with what intent. Hence, McLuhan's "the medium is the message," which means the medium itself, not its content, is the determinant of the outcomes of its use.

Another fundamental statement representing the basic idea of media ecology belongs to John Culkin, who said that "we shape our tools, and

---

[1] McLuhan, Marshall. (1969, March). The Playboy Interview, p. 56.

thereafter our tools shape us." Culkin clarified: "Since our tools are extension of our senses, they shape the way we experience reality."[1]

Mediation predefines the ways humans interact with the environment. Hence, Neil Postman's definition:

> Media ecology looks into the matter of how media of communication affect human perception, understanding, feeling, and value; and how our interaction with media facilitates or impedes our chances of survival.
>
> The word ecology implies the study of environments: their structure, content, and impact on people. <...>
>
> Media ecology is the study of media as environments.[2]

Lance Strate, one of the founders of the Media Ecology Association, stated that media create a range of opportunities for their use, within which users act. He wrote that,

> A medium is not like a billiard ball, producing its effects by striking another ball. Rather, it is more like the table on which the game is played. Put another way, a medium is not an actor, it is a stage on which human agents play their parts. As environments, media do not determine our actions, but they define the range of possible actions we can take, and facilitate certain actions while discouraging others. [...] In other words, as Neil Postman (2000) has explained, cultures are formed within media, rather than media simply being produced by cultures.[3]

Tools are designed for a user to make some changes to the environment. Any new medium is first introduced as a better tool for some "old" operations with the environment. For example, an ax can hit better than a fist, and Zoom allows communicating better than a phone. However, a new medium then unleashes its own power and "imposes" new media functions that lead to environmental changes. The ax eventually enabled colonization, wars and the warrior culture, and Zoom created a new work

---

[1] Culkin, John. (1967). Each culture develops its own sense ratio to meet the demands of its environment. In *McLuhan: Hot and Cool.* Gerald Stearn (Ed.). New York: New American Library. P. 52.

[2] Postman, Neil. 1970. The reformed English curriculum. In *High School 1980: The Shape of the Future in American Secondary Education.* New York: Pitman. P. 161.

[3] Strate, Lance. (2008). Studying media as media: McLuhan and the media ecology approach. MediaTropes, eJournal, Vol. I, p.135.

culture. Thus, at a certain point of use, a medium, if it has succeeded, starts changing the environment and the users themselves.

The media ecology approach allows for singling out of two phases, or pathways, for a medium as an instrument to turn into a medium as an environmental force.

1) The environmentalization of an instrument begins at the sensory level. An instrument becomes successful when a user starts sensing an operated object and not the operating medium. For example, if a fisherman senses the fish, not the fishing rod, then the rod as a tool has succeeded: the sensorium is readjusted.

2) When a medium's use becomes unrecognizable (meaning essential) for a sufficient number of users, its convenience starts reshaping their modus operandi at the cultural level. After that, a medium turns into an environmental force. The environmentalization of an instrument is complete when a user is not just an individual but a community.

From instrumental to environmental: A sensory pathway

Any instrumental enhancement comes with a "price" humans pay with changes occurring in the body (mind, sensorium). Assessing the price humans pay for media innovation is an incredibly long tradition, dating back to the discussion between the god Theuth and King Thamus in Plato's *Phaedrus*.

Theuth and Thamus discussed what humans would gain from the invention of writing. The god Theuth, the inventor, insisted that humans would enhance their memory and increase their wisdom through writing, while Thamus, the king of Egypt (meaning the king of the entire world, who also impersonates the superior god Ammon), argued that humans would lose their memory, as they would become dependent on external inscriptions instead of developing inner notions and would obtain only a semblance of truth instead of truth; they would also obtain only the "show of wisdom" instead of real wisdom.

Quite within the framework of media ecology, the god-inventor and the king-inspector debated the service and disservice of the new medium, writing, in terms of its impact on human faculties, such as memory and wisdom. Through the externalization of data recording, as we would characterize it now, the function that internal memory once served became better fulfilled. However, the memory itself – the organic human faculty of memorization – declined in use and subsequently deteriorated, thereby impairing the human capacity for wisdom.

Marshall McLuhan described this sensory impact of a medium through the dichotomy of extension–amputation. The technological extensions of the body amplify abilities and intensify the burden of actions on the sensorium to such an extent that it disrupts the pre-existing balance of human perception. Because of this burden, the mental and sensory faculties that are extended outside the body become overloaded. This leads to the "numbing" of the organs or faculties that were previously responsible for executing functions now extended by media, as McLuhan explained in *Understanding Media*.[1] To restore the cohesiveness of perception at the new level, encompassing new extensions, the organism resorts to "a desperate and suicidal autoamputation, as if the central nervous system could no longer depend on the physical organs to be protective buffers against the slings and arrows of outrageous mechanism."[2]

Thus, sensory numbing and amputation (meaning the loss of organs/functions) are the flip side of the "extension of man" by media. McLuhan wrote:

> Any invention or technology is an extension or self-amputation of our physical bodies, and such extension also demands new ratios or new equilibriums among the other organs and extensions of the body.[3]

The idea of atrophy, numbness, and even autoamputation of organs and faculties due to the externalization of their functions through media illustrates the profound impact of instrumental use on the sensorium. Not only does the sensorium adapt to new tools – they completely reshape it. A new interface between the user and the environment becomes a new environment to which the body needs to adapt. We shape our tools, and they reshape us.

---

[1] McLuhan, Marshall. (1994 [1964]). *Understanding Media. The Extensions of Man*. Cambridge, Massachusetts: The MIT Press. P. 42.

[2] Ibid. P.43.

[3] Ibid. P.45.

The reverse effect of media on humans can be observed in all instances where the medium becomes good enough for regular use. For example, the use of fire for cooking changed the biochemical processes in the digestive system, because a part of digestion was externalized into the thermal processing of food by fire.

Interestingly, fire was once the primary feature that distinguished humans from animals, a fact metaphorically reflected in the myths of Prometheus or Kipling's story of Mowgli. Media evolution, represented by Prometheus, once gave fire to humans. But now it has almost completely taken fire away. As technological progress advances, all the functions once performed by fire – such as heating, cooking, lighting, and protection – are now carried out by other technologies, many of which do not involve fire at all. Smoking, perhaps, was the last instance of the mass and routine use of fire, but even it is now being replaced by e-cigarettes. Humans, the fire-using animals, become fireless as they grow into more mediated (more human?) beings. The extension of the human ability to control fire by other technologies "amputated" this skill from the human skillset. We no longer use this Promethean gift; many people today are incapable of starting a campfire even when they have a lighter or matches. Fire, the human-making medium, is gone, which may allude to the fact that media evolution is completing a sort of arc...

Debating writing, Theuth advocated for extension and its gain, while Thamus warned about amputation and its harm. Writing enhanced recording but – and precisely because of this enhancement – amputated a part of the memory functions by recording "data" outside the brain.

The decline of the internal memory has become even more visible since the advance of the Internet and digital gadgets. Cellphones, for example, memorize our friends' phone numbers and, as a result, we do not need to remember them. The function of memorizing phone numbers is executed much more reliably by the extension of this operation in a new medium. However, our bodily/mental ability, which was responsible for this, "weakens" because of it. The smartphone, as a medium, extends and amputates abilities, thereby changing the ratio of senses and skills not just for users but for humankind in general: what is instrumental for the user becomes environmental for the entire species.

The "show of wisdom," as Thamus labeled it, which began with writing, now continues to expand in digital media. Google and Wikipedia quickly became an outsourced but instantly available function of everyone's personal memory and wisdom. This function no longer needs to be fulfilled internally by our biological processing capacities. Memory's outcomes have been enhanced through outsourcing, but organic memory is becoming less engaged and thus less trained, leading to its partial "amputation."

The same applies to wisdom: a digital user need not exert much effort in personally accumulating and processing wisdom, as instant access to collective wisdom is readily available through online search. With this, attention spans are shrinking because, to operate with outsourced memory and digitally stored wisdom, the skill of external browsing rather than internal diligence is required. Consequently, the reduction in attention spans weakens the individual's ability to focus longer on a single task for deeper insight.

The average individual's intellectual capacity, as King Thamus warned, may decrease in these circumstances. However, the collective intelligence, as Theuth might argue, increases tremendously. Additionally, the nature of individual intelligence is changing as it becomes more emotional and adept at multitasking, and less rational and diligent.

Social media has replaced a part of the mental and psychological abilities that were responsible for socializing. Algorithms have enhanced socialization through automatization. They gather all of a person's friends in one place, suggest potential friends, prioritize certain friends' posts in the news feed, remind of friends' birthdays, and so on. The very skill of socializing has been extended and mostly outsourced into the new medium. Simultaneously, the individual's necessity to make friends offline decreases and, therefore, the individual skills of making friends, especially in the younger generations, are becoming numb, if not already amputated.

The impact of this media effect on human abilities and, in a broader sense, on the sensorium is incredible, considering the number of connections made available through social media. Socialization has overcome physical limits. However, this global enhancement of human socialization comes with a price. One of the most harmful consequences of digitally accelerated socialization is polarization.[1] Precisely because social media are an extremely successful instrument of socialization, they impact

---

[1] Mir, Andrey. (2020). *Postjournalism and the Death of Newspapers. The Media after Trump: Manufacturing Anger and Polarization*. P. 322.

the perception and skills and, therefore, become an environmental force that changes people and society.

Thus, when a medium is successful, its sensory effect leads to a cultural effect.

From instrumental to environmental: A cultural pathway

The cultural pathway of a medium from instrumental use to environmental force relates formally to the scale of its use. The individual instrumental use of a new medium rebalances the sensorium of the user, as the new interface becomes a new environment for this user. However, when many users adopt this new medium, their individual interfaces-as-environments overlap and amplify each other to the extent of becoming a terraforming force.

When used by a person, a fence is an instrument to protect and defend, a further extension of the skin, beyond clothes and huts. However, when used by a culture, a fence is an environmental force that transforms a nomadic tribe into a sedentary culture and eventually leads to urban civilization reshaping the planet. Similarly, what seemed to be just the instrumental use of a medium in an isolated act (or a series of acts) becomes an environmental force when the user is not an individual but an entire culture.

As McLuhan noted in *The Medium Is the Massage*,

> All media work us over completely. They are so pervasive in their personal, political, economic, aesthetic, psychological, moral, ethical, and social consequences that they leave no part of us untouched, unaffected, unaltered. The medium is the message. Any understanding of social and cultural change is impossible without a knowledge of the way media work as environments.[1]

The cultural impact of the material characteristics of media (the transition of the sensory into the cultural) was first revealed by Harold Innis, a forerunner of media ecology. In *Empire and Communications*

---

[1] McLuhan, Marshall, and Fiore, Quentin. (1967). *The medium is the massage: An inventory of effects*. New York, London and Toronto: Bantam Books. P. 26.

(1950), Innis argued that stones with hieroglyphs or clay tablets, being durable and heavy and, therefore, time-biased media, underlay the rigid and hierarchical Egyptian and Sumer civilizations. On the other hand, light and easily transported papyrus, a space-biased medium that was "suited to wide areas in administration and trade,"[1] allowed the civilization using it to expand through territories, as in the case of Rome. He stated that,

> Materials which emphasize time favour decentralization and hierarchical types of institutions, while those which emphasize space favour centralization and systems of government less hierarchical in character.[2]

The cultural pathway from the instrumental use to the environmental impact of media can be best explored using the example of the phonograph. Marshall McLuhan devoted an entire chapter of *Understanding Media* to the phonograph. He started from the sensory characteristics of this medium as an instrument. In the chapter's subtitle, he called it "The toy that shrank the national chest." He called the phonograph "an extension and amplification of the voice that may well have diminished individual vocal activity, much as the car had reduced pedestrian activity."[3]

Interestingly, McLuhan pointed out that "...the phonograph was involved in many misconceptions, as one of its early names – gramophone – implies." In fact, Edison expected that his invention could be used as a dictation machine in offices, a repeater of teachers' instructions in classrooms, or a "telephone repeater," somewhat similar to today's voicemail. So, the phonograph as an instrument was intended to record speech as it sounds, phonetically. However, this instrumental expectation was transcended by the environmental outcome of this medium's use. The phonograph became "a means of access to all the music and speech of the world", as McLuhan noted.[4]

The example of the phonograph shows that a new medium is always expected to enhance some old functions but instead creates, even imposes, new ones. The phonograph was supposed to enhance (or replace, as a

---

[1] Innis, Harold. 1950. *Empire and Communications*. Oxford: Clarendon Press. P. 7.

[2] Ibid. P. 7.

[3] McLuhan, Marshall. (1994 [1964]). *Understanding Media. The Extensions of Man*. Cambridge, Massachusetts: The MIT Press. P. 275.

[4] Ibid. P. 277.

better alternative) dictation/stenography, teaching, and telephone conversation. It might have achieved some of this, but the true and most powerful effect of the phonograph related to its environmental impact, not its instrumental use.

What was the environmental potential of the phonograph that went unrecognized by its inventor and early users? This is the central question of media ecological analysis: What environmental force is unleashed by this medium as an instrument when its collective use grows large enough? We can try to extend McLuhan's analysis of the phonograph by answering this question.

The case of the phonograph clearly illustrates the transition from the instrumental to the environmental. The phonograph detached audial entertainment from the time and space of performance. Edison created the instrument that emancipated audial entertainment from the constraints of time and space. Listening to musical and vocal performances became transportable, storable, and marketable.

At this point, a new medium undergoes a test of social scalability. How many users will willingly join the use of it? The process is viral: the new instrumental affordance attracts more users, who in turn cause it to proliferate further.

The environmental force that came with the phonograph transcended its instrumental use and the phonograph itself. The detachment of entertainment from the time and space of performance entailed the emergence of a sequence of similar media, such as radio, the record player, or the tape recorder. As McLuhan noticed, "it was radio that finally injected a full electric charge into the world of the phonograph."[1]

A new, virtual, and accessible venue for musical performance emerged. The growing number of users creates the demand for content production specific to this medium. These new wineskins, at first made for old wine – recording oral speech – then required a new wine: the production of performance recordings. The collective use of recordings – instead of listening to live performance – did not replace performances but increased their number to produce even more records and extend their reach, involving ever more artists, producers, and consumers.

[1] McLuhan, Marshall. (1994 [1964]). *Understanding Media. The Extensions of Man.* Cambridge, Massachusetts: The MIT Press. P. 281.

This created the craft and industry of music recording. Distribution increased, competition was boosted, selection broadened, and an industrial market for singers and musicians appeared. A musical revolution started that brought about jazz, the foxtrot, crooners (a by-product of the invention of the microphone, a derivative of the phonograph's "instrumental" development), and all the genres and styles of what later became pop music.

Commercial distribution extended social proliferation. The electrical venue for performances turned out to be much more democratic than the physical one. The mass market appeared: not only the middle class and upper class, but also the masses joined in listening to performances. This, too, affected the specificity of content production. Show business, a child of recorded music and the mass market, emerged.

Long story short: Edison begat the phonograph, the phonograph begat listening freed from the time and space of performance, emancipated listening begat the recording industry, the recording industry begat popular music, popular music begat show business, show business begat fandom culture, fandom culture begat the cult of celebrity, and the cult of celebrity begat Trump.[1]

It can be called the media "butterfly effect" – Edison wanted to merely record oral speech, and this somehow ended in Trump's presidency.

One could perceive Trump's presidency as an accidental fluctuation in the force fields of media evolution. This, however, was not an accident. Trump, or a Trump-like politician, was as much an inevitable outcome of the phonograph's development (or whatever could have come in this media-ecological niche – the recording and broadcasting of music and vocal performances), as Hitler was a logical outcome of radio (the idea first expressed by McLuhan in *Understanding Media*) and Luther was a logical outcome of the printing press.

The logic behind the sequence of environmental events that led from the invention of the phonograph to the election of Trump was well-known

---

[1] As the New York Times wrote, "'Apprentice' celebrity fueled a myth that propelled him to the White House ... His genius, it turned out, wasn't running a company. It was making himself famous – Trump-scale famous – and monetising that fame". – McIntire, Mike, Buettner, Russ, and Craig, Susanne. (2020, September 28). The President's taxes. *The New York Times*.

to both founders of media ecology. Marshall McLuhan wrote in *Understanding Media*:

> In [Edison's] own case, his determination to give the phonograph, like the telephone, a direct practical use in business procedures led to his neglect of the instrument as a means of entertainment. Failure to foresee the phonograph as a means of entertainment was really a failure to grasp the meaning of the electric revolution in general. In our time we are reconciled to the phonograph as a toy and a solace; but press, radio, and TV have also acquired the same dimension of entertainment. Meantime, entertainment pushed to an extreme becomes the main form of business and politics.[1]

Neil Postman devoted his main work *Amusing Ourselves to Death: Public Discourse in the Age of Show Business* (1985) to the effect that television had on culture and politics. Television can be seen as one of the phonograph's successors as "a means of access to all the music and speech of the world" (McLuhan). Postman stated that politicians, including presidents, became entertainers because of television. They focus more on how they impress than on what they do. He wrote:

> Our priests and presidents, our surgeons and lawyers, our educators and newscasters need worry less about satisfying the demands of their discipline than the demands of good showmanship. Had Irving Berlin changed one word in the title of his celebrated song, he would have been as prophetic, albeit more terse, as Aldous Huxley. He need only have written, "There's No Business But Show Business."[2]

The case of the phonograph shows that the use of the instrument for speech recording does more than just record speech. By detaching sounds from the time and space of their performance, the phonograph creates self-sustaining conditions for new cultural practices, which reshape society in a certain way. This is why the study of media use is the question of ecology and not just of communication.

---

[1] McLuhan, Marshall. (1994 [1964]). *Understanding Media. The Extensions of Man.* Cambridge, Massachusetts: The MIT Press. P. 277.

[2] Postman, Neil. (2005 [1985]). *Amusing ourselves to death: Public discourse in the age of show business.* Kindle ed. New York: Penguin Publishing Group. Kl 1721.

The question of responsibility for media effects

Within the instrumental approach to media effects, the role of the phonograph in shaping a pop culture that thereafter impacted public life and politics may raise a question regarding the role of Edison. Is Edison responsible for Trump?

Interestingly, the question of the responsibility of the media inventor/producer, as odd as it may seem, is not that new or unusual. King Thamus condemned the invention of the god Theuth, writing, pointing to the harm this invention would bring to human wisdom. The inventor, who insisted on the benefit of his invention, was warned about the forthcoming harm of his invention. It did not stop writing, however, from proliferating and providing both its services and disservices. As Postman wrote: "We may learn from Thamus the following: once a technology is admitted, it plays out its hand; it does what it is designed to do."[1] Theuth can be blamed, but it neither stops writing from proliferating nor changes its effects: writing does what is in its nature.

The distinction between the instrumental use and the environmental force brings a new perspective in evaluating the responsibility for media effects. When harm is done by an environmental force, it is hard to assign any agency to it. An environmental force emerges from the medium's, not the user's, "behavior."

The "instrumental vs. environmental" analysis can be applied to any medium to place it within the framework of a legal assessment of guilt and responsibility. For example, cars in instrumental use and cars as an environmental force can cause different consequences in terms of defining responsibility for their media effect.

1) The instrumental effect of the car is simple: as an extension of human legs, it is a means of transportation. In the case of harm done, it is also quite simple to define guilt and responsibility: it lies with either the producer or the user of the car.

2) The environmental view of the media effect caused by the car is much more sophisticated. The car formed the entire new economy. Cars entailed the creation of the highway grid, which caused the development of

---

[1] Postman, Neil. (2005 [1985]). *Amusing ourselves to death: Public discourse in the age of show business.* Kindle ed. New York: Penguin Publishing Group. Kl 130.

the highway service infrastructure and the decline of the previous infrastructure with all its accompanying subcultures, such as traditional inns. Cars increased the economic and geopolitical significance of oil and contributed to the economic prosperity of some Middle East states. Cars changed urban settings, created new suburbs and suburban malls, and, therefore, new retail logistics and merchandising. Cars created a completely new experience of sexual relations for an entire generation in the 1950s and later. And so on and so forth.

Now: who is responsible for all of this? It is possible to discuss historical and cultural responsibility, but who is to blame for, say, the demise of traditional inns or the sexual liberation facilitated by the car? Cars changed human conditions, and if we see this change as harmful, where should we draw the line of legal responsibility and to whom should we assign this responsibility?

The duality of the instrumental and environmental views of media creates an even more complex legal dilemma when applied to the Internet. A user can be seen as responsible when he or she calls for violence and uses social media as an amplifier of criminal intentions. However, who is responsible for an environment that favors polarization and where any message, good or bad, tends to drift to the extremes of expression? Is Mark Zukerberg responsible for the effects of Facebook in the same way as Thamus held Theuth responsible for the effects of writing?

The situation becomes even more complicated when the media producers are the media owner. While their "environmental responsibility" remains debatable, a new instrumental dimension appears – the dimension of using media as an instrument for profit extraction. A new category of agency may appear: the "owner" of a media environment, the one who profits from it, who can control it, and, therefore, can adjust environmental settings, including restricting or allowing someone's access. The owner of the environment – a sort of new take on the term "landlord" – can certainly be held responsible for the specific policies enforced in this environment – provided that we understand the true media effects of these policies.

In a sense, digital environments can be seen as human-made premises with their constructors, engineers, owners, and maintenance staff, whose liabilities can be relatively easily defined. The exploration of this perspective may become particularly important as more and more human activities move into the digital environments.

However, the extrapolation of "real estate property management" norms to the digital environment needs to be checked for their applicability. People might have control over rules and policies within digital premises, but the way these premises affect human lives also reflects the nature of the premises themselves. Digital premises ***have to*** be designed in a certain way simply to exist – to sustain themselves.

The design features of social media may seem to be created on a specific platform by a particular inventor. But the essence, the primary media effect of ***any*** social media platform, is the acceleration of users' socialization – in the same way as the essence of the phonograph was the detachment of sounds from the time and space of performance. To repeat Postman's words, "... once a technology is admitted, it plays out its hand; it does what it is designed to do". To change its essential design means to reverse the technology itself.

Accelerated socialization is the greatest and most human-oriented service provided by media throughout all of history because it allows for self-actualization through others, which is the highest value in Maslow's hierarchy of needs. The mechanisms of virality and relevance that made Facebook such an amazing tool are also the exact same mechanisms that sustain the platform's ad business and, therefore, the platform's very existence.

Unfortunately, but unavoidably, the accelerated and automated socialization on social media leads to more noise and more effort needed to overcome this noise. Eventually, the amplification of extremes and polarization become inevitable side effects of this dependency between better self-actualization and better ad-targeting on Facebook and other social media in general.[1]

Thus, the same environmental force – artificially accelerated personal engagement – is behind both the service and disservice of this medium. The service of self-actualization through others on social media is maintained by profit extraction, which, in a sense, is an institutional maintenance fee society pays for this service – much like how the monopolization of the agenda by institutions and corporations was the

---

[1] See: Mir, Andrey. (2020). *Postjournalism and the Death of Newspapers. The Media after Trump: Manufacturing Anger and Polarization*. P. 335.

maintenance fee paid by society for the service journalism provided to democracy.

The question of regulation

Technically, it is quite possible to impose restrictions on users' self-actualization on a specific platform. The recent bans of Trump and his supporters by Facebook and Twitter proved that a concrete platform, as long as it is managed by a corporate entity, can be responsive to political demands. However, the attempts to minimize the disservice also minimize the service, and therefore the convenience and appeal of the medium. The regulatory restrictions, even if technically possible, weaken the maintenance mechanism of this specific platform and create opportunities for alternatives – here, media ecology approximates political economy. The environmental force will find release through other media devices of this niche, such as Discord, Parler, Telegram, or some other, yet-to-be-created platform.

Paradoxically, regulation might affect a specific platform but not the environmental force that this platform embodies. The name of the media device or the personality of its inventor does not matter. What matters is that the social media platforms maintain and develop themselves by extracting value from users' engagement. Otherwise, the platforms would deteriorate and yield the space to others. The environmental niche itself would inevitably be filled with platforms that perform this function through this mechanism. Furthermore, the restrictions of self-expression on social media risk turning into the endless cat-and-mouse regulation game of censorship, which might lead to consequences much worse for democracy than the harm they are intended to regulate.

The disservice of a medium cannot be removed without disrupting its service. In the logic of media ecology, the interference of human agency in environmental forces hardly reverses or cancels the effects of those forces but rather creates new environmental forces with new effects. Therefore, a new or a newly disturbed balance of forces appear, in which benevolence to users is neither guaranteed nor predictable. By default, it can be stated that regulation of the media environment does not "fix" the media environment but creates a new and different one, in which the "fixed" service will be accompanied by a new disservice.

The simple example: the introduction of political regulation and censorship on social media platforms after the January 6 U.S. Capitol Attack in 2021 did not suppress the dissent in society but rather gives proof of suppression and evokes the reinforced release of this dissent through other channels/platforms. The environmental force that accelerates user engagement for the users' socialization and the platforms' profit will always tend to abandon the platforms with higher regulatory pressure and move toward the platforms with lower regulatory pressure. If this happens, a regulatory zeal will produce grey zones or even "black markets" of self-actualization, just because this environmental force, already unleashed, will search for an alternative release.

This means that such regulatory interference will create new environmental forces and may lead to effects that are the opposite to those intended. The most probable outcome will be that spontaneous amateur dissent will mobilize into a full-fledged political force or even an organized conspiracy, the direct product of suppression. What might be seen as a solution for a platform will become a new trigger for the media environment as a whole. The only way to put the toothpaste back into the tube is to establish nearly total control over society's behavior, which is politically impossible in the West (except for its inherently digital variant, social scoring, which seems to be successfully emerging in the East).

Nevertheless, the zeal to regulate social media as an instrument, neglecting its environmental nature, exists and will persist. The explanation for this regulatory activity lies not only in the lack of ecological understanding of media but also in the fact that such regulation is a good business. A form of regulatory capture emerges: those profiting from regulation and censorship benefit directly from what they regulate and censor. For them, political division is not a bug, it's the condition of business. Their own competence in capitalizing on regulation becomes the sole measure of their efficiency. Such regulation will likely exacerbate rather than resolve the issues it aims to tackle.

To make an even more radical statement: any regulation of the media environment aimed at modifying the behavior of "others", if efficient at all, inevitably leads to new disturbances in the environmental forces, and the effect will always be the opposite of what is intended. The more, or even the only, effective approach to regulating environment is regulating one's own behavior, not the behavior of "others". This approach lies, of course, in the area of media education and media literacy. As history shows, the powerful always tried to restrict "others" in their use of writing or printing, but eventually, it was literacy that helped society to adjust – after certain price for the changes was paid, of course.

Considerations of this kind lead to a conclusion that can frame two approaches to the responsibility for media use and the possibility of media regulation.

1) When the instrumental approach is not distinguished from the environmental one, media tend to be judged as a simple amplifier of an agency behind the media use, with a tendency for this agency to be seen as evil. This approach unavoidably ends in prosecutorial bias and political censorship.

2) When the instrumental and environmental approaches are distinguished, the necessity emerges to limit the responsibility for a media effect to instrumental use and, therefore, to the user, producer, or owner. At the same time, the most impactful cultural force of media relates to their environmental effect, for which producers, owners, or users of media cannot be held responsible. The environmental effects of media should be dealt with outside of the concepts of guilt or personal responsibility, because an environmental force has no user, producer, or agency. An environment is indifferent to regulation by its inhabitants but can accommodate their adaptation. For dealing with the media environment, media literacy is the key.

The regulation of new media brings unprecedented challenges. In the digital environment, the instrumentality of media swallows the user. A medium has become not just an environmental force but an environment in the literal sense. We act and live inside the instrument. To grasp the oddity of this condition, one can imagine a caveman resettling into a stone ax.

Probe: A brief chart of media effects

Media effects of...

- ✓ Speech: the self-domestication of man
- ✓ Writing: making public issues
- ✓ Alphabet: making personal duties a public issue
- ✓ Print: making class struggle a public issue
- ✓ Electricity: making remote issues a public issue
- ✓ Digital: making personal identity a public issue[1]

Speech: the self-domestication of man

Speech accompanied and provided a delay in the response to environmental triggers. Naming things allowed for deliberation and communication. The delay in response required for this was detrimental for humans as animals, but it allowed the accumulation of individual and collective efforts in time and space at a level unobtainable for other animals. The strategy proved to be beneficial evolutionarily and eventually divorced humans from the animal kingdom.

Deliberation and cooperation also changed the social structure of primordial humans. According to some anthropologists, speech allowed beta-males to conspire against and kill alpha-males. This entailed a social revolution: communication diversified the ways of challenging power in the group. Physical strength ceased to be the decisive factor for procreation and leadership. The strongest ones started to be dependent on the support of the smartest ones; politics emerged. The harem-type family led by the strongest and most violent male grew to become a larger social unit led by the hierarchy of the strongest and savviest males, who shared resources, power and responsibility for communal well-being. The zoological violence and instinctive protectiveness transitioned to meritocracy and care. Herd became tribe. Thus, speech domesticated men at the levels of sensory reactions and social organization.

---

[1] The essay is based on the "probe" with the same title in *New Explorations: Studies in Culture and Communication*, 3(1).

Writing: making public issues

Writing emerged as a tool of bookkeeping and taxation for the temple bureaucracy in the first irrigation civilizations. Irrigation provided a production surplus and thus invoked the necessity of accounting. The recording of divine/celestial events responsible for the river level proved to be a source of power. With writing, shamans became priests and magic turned into religion. Thus, irrigation is the mother of writing, and the bureaucrat is the second oldest profession.

The recording of incomes and celestial events maintained the privilege of the temple bureaucracy as a managerial class. To secure class privilege, schools and libraries emerged that accumulated and reproduced the cadres and the monopoly of knowledge. Teaching literacy required reflection on the nature of writing and language. The priests became scholars. Preserving texts in the libraries required classification. The taxonomy of knowledge emerged, followed by the division of disciplines, from architecture and taxation to cosmogony and astronomy. Thus, the necessity to secure the class privilege of the priest-scribes made public matters the object of contemplation. This is why the effect of writing is making public issues.

Alphabet: making personal duties a public issue

The alphabet detached the signs of writing from their resemblance to nature and thereby completed the abstraction of writing.

The divorce of writing from mimicking nature enabled the comprehension of the abstract Absolute, the pure idea that has no resemblance nor any connection to perceivable reality. The communities that developed the first alphabets, the ancient Semites, came up with the idea of a single deity as the ultimate cause of all natural and supernatural forces. The alphabet facilitated monotheism (Logan[1]). Under polytheism, various forces ruled the world, allowing truth to be negotiated. Under monotheism, truth is the Absolute given by the sole God and therefore must be followed.

---

[1] Logan, Robert K. (2004). *The Alphabet Effect: A Media Ecology Understanding of the Making of Western Civilization*. Cresskill NJ: Hampton Press (1st edition 1986. New York: Wm. Morrow).

Religion turned from a collective practical enterprise into an individual moral obligation. Communal togetherness split into personal duties controlled by God and society. This is why the effect of the alphabet is making personal duties a public issue.

Print: making class struggle a public issue

Printing freed scholars and scribes from the slavish job of copying, thus emancipating countless literate man-hours that could now be used to record new content.

Recording current events and ideas became a habit and duty in the *Respublica Literaria*, a virtual international college of learned men in Medieval Europe. The exchange of news turned into the business and industry of journalism. The increased news supply accelerated trade and entrepreneurship. Print also made the Bible affordable for individual study and interpretation. This weakened the political power of the Church. Thus, economic and political conditions appeared for the emergence of a new class, the bourgeoisie.

Journalism satisfied the demand for business news but also provided the bourgeoisie with a tool for political claims. The class struggle of the bourgeoisie with the aristocracy and clergy led to the development of democracy and capitalism. The further development of capitalism created a new class: the proletariat. The self-identification and political claims of the proletariat also relied on printing production and journalism. Bourgeois and worker revolutions marked the age of printing. This is why the effect of print is making class struggle a public issue.

Electricity: making remote issues a public issue

Electricity enabled the instant delivery of distant news, bringing international affairs into the local news agendas.

The telegraph and especially radio bridged space on a planetary scale. This led to clashes among global empires over spheres of political influence and resource control. However, while radio enabled industrial all-out wars, culminating in the two World Wars, television quickly ended the era of full-scale industrial wars by affecting human empathy through images of hostilities. In the era of television, wars turned into hybrid military operations or commercial, political, and regulatory conflicts.

Either way, the instant delivery of distant news enabled globalization, which means electricity made remote issues a public issue.

Digital: making personal identity a public issue

Digital media emancipated authorship by giving billions of people access not just to information but to presenting themselves to the world.

Human widespread engagement on the Internet, the blogosphere, and then social media opened up new economic opportunities. The personal data and time spent on digital platforms became commodities for the platform owners. Seeking better engagement, platforms train the algorithms and the entire environment of response, including other users, to pay more attention to the identity signals of users. The amplification of identity signalling serves both the user's unconscious desire for response and the business needs of the platform. The hyper-focus on identity is an inevitable feature of a digital society. This is why the effect of digitalization is making personal identity a public issue.

Back to tribal truth: the digital orality of the global village

How digital orality reshapes the epistemology of truth[1]

Phone-phobia of the phone-based communication

Jonathan Haidt's book *The anxious generation: How the great rewiring of childhood is causing an epidemic of mental illness* has sparked debates about digital harm. Haidt advocates for a return from a "phone-based" childhood to a "play-based" childhood. Curiously, however, phone-addicted youths are actually also phone-phobic: Millennials and Gen Zers do not like to call and talk. They prefer texting.

The flip from calling to texting as the primary use of phones happened sometime in the early 2010s. As studies show, before 2011–2014, most smartphone users still preferred calling. But then texting surpassed calling.[2]

The primary motive for this appears to be the unspoken desire of users, especially youngsters – digital natives – to remain physically isolated while digitally connected. This is exactly what smartphones allow and incentivize. A 2016 study showed that 76% of those aged 18–34 deemed texting more convenient, while 63% found it less disruptive than voice calls.[3] Since then, this preference has grown into an anxiety that young people experience when someone calls them or when they need to call someone. Smartphones function as social semiconductors – they give the user more control over being "alone together."

---

[1] The essay is based on the paper "Digital orality" presented at the conference "Orality and literacy in an age of social media" at Geneva College, Beaver Falls, PA, on April 5, 2024.

[2] See, for example: Smith, Aaron. (2011, September 19). Americans and text messaging. *Pew Research Center*. and Newport, Frank. (2014, November 10). The new era of communication among Americans. *Gallup*.

[3] Why millennials still love text. (2017). *OpenMarket*.

The widespread utilization of texting on devices primarily designed for talking seemingly signifies the onset of a new era of literacy, now based on digital rather than printed text. But no, despite the formal use of letters, it's not literacy. It enables instant conversational reactions similar to oral exchange. Inheriting technologically and historically from print literacy, digital texting inaugurated a new era of orality – digital orality.

Television and the rediscovery of orality

For a long time, orality was understood as illiteracy or seen as a matter of folklore and anthropology. This changed in the 1950–60s, when the explosion of electronic media spurred the development of media studies. At that time, radio was still perceived as a new medium. Cinema and sound recording, too, were in a stage of constant innovation. They all were modern things. All of a sudden, an even newer medium, television, emerged. The profound effect of electronic media prompted Marshall McLuhan, Neil Postman and others to look for patterns and analogies in the past. McLuhan contrasted the effects of electronic media with print and discovered the Gutenberg Galaxy.

The "comparative studies" of print and electronic media drew scholars' attention further to the cultural effects of orality and literacy. Walter Ong wrote:

> Our understanding of the differences between orality and literacy developed only in the electronic age, not earlier. Contrasts between electronic media and print have sensitized us to the earlier contrast between writing and orality.[1]

Eric Havelock noticed that, in the span of just 12 months in 1962 and 1963, five fundamental works on literacy and orality were published: Levi-Strauss' *La Pensee Sauvage*, Goody and Watt's *The Consequences of Literacy*, McLuhan's *The Gutenberg Galaxy*, Mayr's *Animal Species and Evolution*, and his own *Preface to Plato*.[2] He labeled this explosion of interest "the modern discovery of orality." Basically, this all occurred

[1] Ong, Walter. 2002 [1982]. *Orality and Literacy*. P. 2.

[2] Havelock, Eric. (1986). *The Muse Learns to Write. Reflections on Orality and Literacy from Antiquity to the Present*. P. 25.

because of television and the cultural disturbances it produced. As Havelock put it:

> Since, as literates, we have only very recently woken up to the presence of orality as a contemporary fact in our midst, revived in the electronic media, there need not be surprise if this provokes a new look at what may have been the role of orality in ancient Greece.[1]

Walter Ong further developed this idea in his 1982 *Orality and Literacy*: "In this diachronic framework, past and present, Homer and television, can illuminate one another."[2] So, as soon as media scholars were triggered by the effect of television and started exploring the relations between TV and print, the effects of other media eras began to be recognized.

Figure 29. "In this diachronic framework, past and present, Homer and television, can illuminate one another." (Walter Ong)

[1] Havelock, Eric. (1986). *The Muse Learns to Write. Reflections on Orality and Literacy from Antiquity to the Present.* P. 118.

[2] Ong, Walter. 2002 [1982]. *Orality and Literacy*. P. 2.

Orality and literacy are not just ways of passing and storing information. They represent two contrasting states of mind and culture. Before writing, an individual received environmental signals simultaneously-from-around, in the fashion of hearing, which led McLuhan to call this sensory mode "acoustic space." Writing, on the contrary, engages only vision while numbing all other senses, favoring the so-called visual bias, or "visual space," in McLuhan's term.

Unlike the spherical space of hearing, visual space allows the isolation of one sense – the sense of vision – thus creating an affordance for sensory and, consequently, mental focus. Eventually, with the development of writing, the sensory capacity of vision produced a cognitive faculty of inner vision – the ability to isolate "things" from the environment and focus on them. Such mental focus on both external objects and their reflections in our perception was not typical of the oral mind.

As soon as affordance for focusing emerges, it diverts cognitive effort from multitasking. Unlike the acoustic mode of perception with its spherical and simultaneous input, visual bias requires things to be comprehended one at a time, sequentially and linearly. Writing trains the brain not only to focus on certain things but also to structure them in a certain sequence. Sequencing encourages prioritizing, and prioritizing encourages the agency of a person comprehending the world. This is why literacy historically led to the emergence of theorizing, abstract logic, and individualism. In orality, a person is immersed in the "here-and-now" environment, whereas in literacy, a person is detached from the environment and is capable of mentally operating without the environment at all. What were reflexes for the oral mind turned into reflections in the literate mind.

Writing did not end or replace orality with literacy but rather created the conditions for their complex interplay. Orality, or the residues of orality, as Walter Ong called them, continue to exert significant influence over various aspects of individual and public activities. These oral residues retain substantial regulatory power, such as employing formulaic expressions to instigate or resolve conflicts or to facilitate cooperation. In many situations, when social dynamics are regulated by oral communication, people revert to orality. A vivid example of oral residue in a literate society is the mafia. Fraternities, collectives of hobbyists, field worker groups, expeditions, political debates, prisons, and the entire Gulag

Archipelago, along with some other social or professional groups or activities, still exhibit the features of residual orality to varying degrees.

Orality has not only survived within the conditions of literacy but also reemerged in a new form after electronic media enabled the transmission of spoken language. Walter Ong called this new form "secondary orality" [1] and distinguished it from "primary orality" – the orality of minds and cultures unaffected by writing.

Besides being an effect of electronic media, secondary orality also inevitably represented the oral speech of highly literate societies, where people's brains were already trained in literacy for at least several generations. Therefore, despite its oral format, secondary orality was affected by the conventions of written speech. In contrast to primary orality, the secondary orality of electronic culture tended to employ written vocabulary and syntax as well as represent the linear and sequential thinking fostered by print literacy.

Digital hybridization of speech

As was the case with television in the time of McLuhan and Postman, digital media turned the attention of media ecologists, once again, to past media epochs in a search for patterns and analogies. But now, thanks to Innis, McLuhan, Postman, Havelock, and Ong, we are better equipped to see media effects of orality, literacy, and what is coming after, with the new medium – digital media.

Digital media enabled a new communication phenomenon: digital speech. It began with hyperlinks. Unlike the linear development of written narrative, which leaves the reader no choice but to follow it, hyperlinks made it possible for "reading" to wander, akin to the spontaneous development of oral conversation. The cognitive discipline of Gutenberg's shackles was broken: a reader's mind could now travel from one "text" to another while still "reading" from the same surface of the screen.

Then, mobile phones and the blogosphere made oral-like conversational exchange possible through written (typed) symbols. Enabled by new media, interactive written speech emerged. Smartphones and social media completed the advancement of digital speech. Nowadays,

[1] Ong, Walter. (2002 [1982]). *Orality and Literacy*. P. 11.

most people communicate by typing almost as much as they talk and certainly more than they write.

Digital speech combines elements of both oral and written communication. Like oral speech, digital speech permits the instant exchange of replies; like writing, it leaves behind a record and can be transmitted across time and space, thus involving more people than just immediate interlocutors.

There are some other key characteristics of oral and written speech that digital speech synthesizes into a new blend.

The syntax of digital speech. In oral speech, interlocutors collaboratively develop the thema-rhematic structure by passing the thema (subject) to each other and adding the rhema (new information on the subject) in turn. Each utterance becomes the rhema for the previous one and serves as the thema for the subsequent one. Interlocutors cooperate and rely on each other to construct the syntax structure of their conjoined discourse.

In written speech, phrases cannot rely on something previously said by someone else. Instead, written speech follows its own syntactic structure, typical of a monologue. Written sentences do not require thema-rhematic prompts, as they are self-reliant. But this demands that the writer deliberate more on words and their order, considering not only what to write about but also how to write it. These imperceptible yet significant cognitive efforts not only render written speech structurally self-sufficient but also better organized and thought out.

Digital speech is formally conversational and employs thema-rhematic principles of dialogue when the interlocutors prompt each other to respond. But it is also written (typed) individually on a device and thus its production is isolated and self-immersed, as in writing. This dialogue-monologue confusion, enabled by the very materiality of the digital medium, often leads to a well-known effect of social media: the interlocutors do not really "listen" to each other. Due to isolated speech production (typing on one's own digital device), thema-rhematic prompts in digital communication may not foster cooperation but instead contribute to the disintegration of dialogic speech.

Speech as behaviour and digital "verbomotorics." Oral speech is a muscular activity. It involves not only the articulation of sounds but also signalling through emotions, tones, vocalization, gestures, facial expressions, and other extralinguistic means. To describe orality, Ong used the notion of the "verbomotor lifestyle." He borrowed the term *verbomoteur* from French anthropologist Marcel Jousse, who studied mimicry, rhythms, and gestures as mnemotechnics in oral cultures.[1] Because of its verbomotor nature, oral speech is not solely a linguistic phenomenon but rather a behavioral one. Some psycholinguists, following the ideas of Lev Vygotsky, describe oral speech as "speech-behavior." Verbomotorics can be explained as the indivisible unity of speech and behavior, which includes muscular activities that carry symbolic meaning and accompany oral speech.

Writing and reading, too, involve some "muscular" activity, such as moving a pen or eyeballs; however, unlike gestures or vocalizations in oral speech, the muscular activities of writing do not carry symbolic meanings.

Similarly to writing, digital speech involves the "meaningless" muscular activity of typing-and-tapping; however, it also incorporates some verbomotor features of oral speech, converting them into digital forms: emojis, abbreviations as interjections (*LOL*, *OMG*, etc.), caps lock as typographic YELLING or, conversely, the dismissal of capital letters and punctuation due to their "passive aggression," etc. To this range, other "digital-verbomotor" means can be added, such as GIFs, reels, visual or verbo-graphic memes, etc. Thus, digital speech retrieves the speech-behavior typical of oral communication but replaces bodily signals with digital substitutions.

Speech as a synchronizer. Serving cooperation, oral speech required synchronization and alignment between the participants. To achieve the desired effects of communication, interlocutors needed to be properly "tuned" into each other. Talking to one another, people synchronized their efforts and defined each other's social statuses, achieving the needed degrees of tribal coherence. In a romantic view of tribal customs, this might be seen as harmony. But in fact, this "harmony" also included a lot of mutual challenging and bullying, which Walter Ong described as the "agonistic mentality" of the oral lifestyle. Oral communication, therefore, served not only for meaning transmission but also for the ratification of statuses.

---

[1] Ong, Walter. (2002 [1982]), *Orality and Literacy*, pp. 66-67.

Linguists describe this as the phatic function of speech. Psychologists would refer to it as establishing rapport. The same function is identified by ethologists as "social grooming." A significant part of our oral interaction involves "social grooming" and establishing rapport: 40–50% of oral interaction is wasted on establishing mutual relationships, reaching nearly 100% in small talk.

In written communication, one doesn't need to establish rapport and therefore can focus solely on meaning and its organization. Of course, letters, manifestos, and other forms of written addresses still require some form of "social grooming" of the reader, but this is more a feature of written communication than writing itself. Writing is inherently reader-blind – it is unconcerned with specific characteristics or the mood of readers at the moment of reading.

Similarly to oral speech and unlike writing, digital speech is a conversational phenomenon. On social media or in messengers, digital speech is aimed at maintaining relations. At the same time, unlike in oral conversation, relation-oriented and status-establishing efforts in digital speech are not transient. They persist and become exposed beyond those involved in immediate conversation. In fact, through their phatic efforts, digital interlocutors seek to affect not only each other (as in oral speech) but also a distant and often imaginary audience (as in written text). Digital speech is impulsive yet not evanescent, thus extending its propensity to affect well beyond the immediate conversation.

In terms of maintaining relationships and tribal integrity, oral speech represented the constant exchange of requests for affirmation. The digital hybrid of speech does the same, with one exception: it knows no physical limits, thus amplifying the endless mutual requests for affirmation across time and space. On social media, conversational requests for affirmation extend beyond the circle of interlocutors and the time of conversation, reaching out to distant others. This digital feature satisfies the highest need in Maslow's hierarchy: the need for self-actualization through others, the most precious added value of social networks. However, with no physical constraints, the limitless opportunity to satisfy this need, along with the low-cost efforts and instant dopamine gratification for the pursuit of belonging, can lead to addiction and agitation. Limitless digital speech, just technically, due to its characteristics as a medium, simply has to ignite the race for affirmation and lead to polarization and hysteria.

These features of oral speech, written speech, and their digital hybrid[1] are represented in a chart (Figure 30).

Digital hybridization of speech

Oral speech	*Written speech*
• Instant exchange (here and now)	• Isolated writing
• Dialogue syntax (thema-rhematic dependency)	• Monologue syntax (thema-rhematic self-reliance)
• The form serves to establish rapport	• The form serves to organize meaning
• Verbomotor intensity (immersive speech-behavior)	• Grammar, semantics
• Impulsive, evanescent	• Deliberate, detached (always not-now)
• Feedback affects the production of meaning	• Feedback doesn't affect the production of meaning

Digital speech

- Instant as communication but isolated as production
- Dialogue-monologue confusion: thema-rhematic disruption of syntax ("parallel talking")
- Impulsive but not evanescent: extends beyond here-and-now
- Verbomotor intensity in the form of digital pantomime (emojis), interjections, memes, reels, etc.
- Between participants but also for a remote audience (rapport disruption, amplified requests for affirmation)

Figure 30. The features of oral and written speech and their digital hybridization.

Discovery of digital orality

Ong's secondary orality was a cognitive and cultural effect of the speech influenced by electronic media. Does the digital hybridization of oral and written speech bring about a new form of orality?

Since the Internet has rekindled interest in orality, media scholars have begun pondering the nature of Internet communication, noting its capacity to merge the features of oral and written speech. Ong's concept of secondary orality inspired Robert Logan, a physics professor at the University of Toronto and co-author of Marshall McLuhan, to coin the term "tertiary orality," which he also referred to as "digital orality." Here is how he introduced the term in 2007:

---

[1] I explored the digital hybridization of speech and its historic roots in: *Digital Future in the Rearview Mirror: Jaspers' Axial Age and Logan's Alphabet Effect*. (2024).

> Walter Ong in his study of orality made a distinction between primary and secondary orality: "I style the orality of a culture totally untouched by any knowledge of writing or print, 'primary orality.' It is 'primary' by contrast with 'secondary orality' of present-day high-technology culture." Based on the conversational nature of the Internet and text-based communication I would like to suggest that there exists a third kind of orality, namely, tertiary or digital orality. Tertiary or digital orality is the orality of emails, blog posts, listservs, instant messages (IM) and SMS, which are mediated paradoxically by written text transmitted by the Internet. [1]

Logan used the term before the proliferation of smartphones and social media, so, at the time, he could not observe in detail the hybridization of oral and written speech into digital speech that occurred when instant texting became the dominant mode of digital communication. His derivation of the "tertiary or digital orality" from Ong's succession of oralities was a pure and genuine insight, the farsighted introduction of a definition, the meaning of which continues to be filled in by the subsequent development of media.

If oral speech was the medium of orality and written speech was the medium of literacy, digital speech is the medium of a new state of mind and culture that can be indeed labeled as digital orality. The use of the term "orality" here should not be confused with the idea of the "oral" production of speech. Oral utterance is a vocal act, indeed, but orality is a cognitive, behavioural, and cultural phenomenon. McLuhan, Havelock, and Ong focused not on phonetics, but on the cognitive and cultural effects of oral speech as a medium. Digital orality is not "oral"; it is an oral-like state of mind and culture enabled by digital speech.

Digital speech rewires our cognitive capacities and cultural setups as any new medium does. To explore changes caused by new media, in the 1970s, McLuhan introduced the so-called Tetrad[2], which described four universal media effects: enhancement, obsoleting, retrieval, and reversal. According to him, any human technology, medium, or artifact:

---

[1] Robert Logan first introduced the term "tertiary or digital orality" in the 2007 article "The emergence of artistic expression and secondary perception" and then developed it in: Logan, Robert. (2010). *Understanding New Media: Extending Marshall McLuhan.* New York: Peter Lang. (Second edition: 2016.)

[2] The Tetrad was first introduced by Marshall McLuhan in the 1970s and described later in: McLuhan, Marshall, and McLuhan, Eric. (1988). *Laws of Media: The New Science.*

1. Enhances something.

2. Makes something obsolescent.

3. Retrieves something from the past that was previously obsolesced.

4. Flips into something opposite or reverses its effect or characteristics when pushed to the limits of its potential.

This Tetrad, or Laws of Media, as McLuhan called it, can be applied to digital media. The effects of enhancement and obsolescence caused by digital media are widely reflected upon – digital media enhance information exchange while rendering offline life obsolete. As for the effects of reversal and retrieval, they are less noticed. By observing digital speech and its capacity to merge the features of writing and oral conversation, it can be seen that digital media reverse some effects of literacy and retrieve some features of orality. To comprehend exactly which effects of orality and literacy are retrieved and reversed, we need to inventory them and consider how their reversal and retrieval might manifest.

In the book *Digital future in the rearview mirror: Jaspers' Axial Age and Logan's Alphabet Effect*,[1] I suggested a list of such features to examine them and see how they play out under the condition of digital orality (Figure 31).

[1] Mir, Andrey. (2024). *Digital Future in the Rearview Mirror: Jaspers' Axial Age and Logan's Alphabet Effect*.

Orality	vs.	Literacy
Environmental immersion		Environmental detachment
Acoustic space: spherical and simultaneous perception		Visual space: linear and sequential perception
Equilibrium of senses: audile-tactile integrity		Isolated vision as a cognitive faculty
Holism and synthesis		Fragmentation and analysis
Syntagmatic connections		Paradigmatic selections
Relation-oriented		Object-oriented
Verbomotor, extralinguistic speech-behaviour		Speech as the actualization of language
Rhythm		Melody
Dialogue		Monologue
Collective immersion		Individualism
Personal exposure		Private space
Bragging		Modesty
Authenticity		Hypocrisy
Agonistic mentality		Tolerance
Mocking		Irony
Customs		Codified law
Situational/analog thinking		Abstract thinking
Presentism		Historism
Answering		Questioning
Wisdom		Thinking
Magic		Rationality
Mythology		Religion, ideology
Negotiated truth		Absolute truth

Figure 31. The features of orality and literacy.

Digital orality: the reversal of truth

In oral communication, meaning is subordinated to practical situational needs. The oral mind is relation-oriented: people interact to optimize relationships in pursuit of social benefits. Unlike relation-oriented orality, literacy is subject-matter-oriented, because writing detached the subject matter from situational circumstances (Havelock's "separation of the knower from the known"[1]) and allowed the subject matter itself to be the focus of contemplation.

Digital orality reverses this setting of the literate mind. Digital communication tends to disregard the subject matter and instead focuses on establishing the mutual statuses of users, thus resembling primary orality. Each action on social media is a covert request for affirmation, regardless of the topic.

According to McLuhan, radio and television tremendously increased people's "empathic involvement" with distant affairs, otherwise utterly irrelevant to the everyday life of an ordinary person. Social media not only amplified that electronic-media effect of involvement with distant news but also boosted people's direct "empathic involvement" with each other.

Everyone on social media seeks validation from others but is also bombarded with countless requests for affirmation from them. This medium makes mutual validation the top priority in human interaction, mirroring the dynamic of tribal community, albeit on a much larger scale – digital tribes expand with no physical limits. In catering to the human struggle for recognition, social media encourage users to sacrifice "objective" content for affirmation. The content of our exchange becomes just an excuse for requesting affirmation from others.

By prioritizing relationships over the subject matter, digital orality has a profound epistemological effect on the perception of truth in everyday life. Historically, truth was seen differently in oral and literate cultures. Immersed in situational living, individuals in primary-oral cultures would negotiate truth with divine patrons or each other: oral truth was situation-dependent and therefore negotiable. Before writing, there was no concept of absolute truth; truth was verified through outcomes, and everyone could try to push for better outcomes. Writing enabled abstract thinking, which led to the emergence of the abstract absolute. One consequence of this was monotheism. Another was the notion of absolute truth. With the development of writing, both the cognitive capacity and the practical need for absolute truth arose, as absolute truth became the foundation of law and knowledge.

---

[1] Havelock, Eric. (1963). *Preface to Plato*. P. 197.

This is being reversed by digital orality, too. Prioritizing the establishment of relationships over adhering to subject matter, digital orality retrieves situational, practical truth. The power of absolute truth diminishes. Truth is becoming situational-dependent and verified by outcomes in digital reality. And since digital reality has no physical feedback – the only environmental feedback comes from others, curated by algorithms – the situational verification of truth is conducted by a sufficient number of others, through their likes, posts, and reposts. So, as anyone can and even is compelled to push for better affirmation outcomes, truth is negotiated again. This inherently tribal epistemological condition of digital orality affects the entire spectrum of human relations, extending beyond the digital – into politics, journalism, and even academia. The hardware of communication determines the epistemological software of culture.

A similar analysis can be applied to the entire range of cognitive and cultural transitions enabled by phonetic literacy 2500 years ago. Long ago, the shift from orality to literacy entailed the move from magic to faith, from superstition to religion, from myth to logos, from polytheism to monotheism, from customs to laws, from moral relativism to the moral absolute, from practical and negotiated truths to objective and absolute truth, from relation-centering to subject-matter-centering, from natural and supernatural "physics" to metaphysics, from the Dionysian to the Apollonian, from the "cycle of life" to personal destiny, from the agitation of tribal belonging to the individual tragedy of (not-)becoming. At the roots of orality was the chanting shaman. At the roots of literacy was the literate priest (and its later iterations: philosopher, scholar, writer, journalist).

Today, digital speech-behavior reverses these effects of literacy and retrieves the environmental and conversational immersion of orality. We can now see what McLuhan implied when he fathomed that electricity "retribalized" society. Secondary, or electronic, orality, ended the environmental detachment of literacy and immersed humans into the shared emotions of the global village. Today, digital orality is completing retribalization, testing our tolerance by bringing others closer and intrusively, much like oral society once did – but now right onto the intimacy of our screens.

Eight theses on digital media literacy

A manifesto of cooperation with the inevitable[1]

1. Media literacy is cooperation with the inevitable

1.1. Media have evolved from implements to environments. One can operate *with* a stone ax – but *within* the Internet. People can harness an instrumental use but not an environmental force.

1.1.1. Media literacy is no longer a technical manual – it's a survival guide.

1.2. Our ability to control media as environmental forces do not exceed our ability to control environments. When the Persian King Xerxes ordered to lash the sea for destroying his pontoon bridge, the sea remained indifferent. But at least Xerxes made it into history.

1.3. Speaking of the sea. To describe our relations with the media environment, Marshall McLuhan used a metaphor borrowed from Edgar Allan Poe's short story *A Descent into the Maelstrom* (1841).

1.3.1. A fishing boat with three brothers was drawn into a mile-wide maelstrom. One brother was swept away by the waves. Another was paralyzed by horror. But the third watched the terrifying spectacle as a manifestation of God's might and was amazed by its structure.

1.3.2. With awe and reverent curiosity, he observed the whirling walls. Suddenly, he noticed that some debris remained afloat in the descending waters. He abandoned the boat and clung to a

[1] The essay is based on the article *Discourse*, titled "The seven essential truths of digital media literacy" (2024, August). Revised for book publication.

barrel. As time passed, the whirlpool subsided, and the sailor was rescued by another boat.

1.3.3. As McLuhan explained, "Sailor saved himself by studying the action of the whirlpool and by co-operating with it... It was this amusement born of his rational detachment as a spectator of his own situation that gave him the thread which led him out of the Labyrinth."

1.4. Media literacy relies on detached observation and pattern recognition. Cooperation with the inevitable is the only prudent strategy when the forces of media gain the might of a maelstrom.

1.5. Media literacy discerns what we do with media from what media do to us. The former is instrumental use, while the latter is an environmental force. No King Xerxes can change the media maelstrom, but it is still possible to affect the conditions of being drawn into it.

2. Media literacy is Internet hygiene

2.1. The myth of the Internet as a giant dump is only half right. It is a dump in the sense that everybody dumps their stuff there; however, far from everything ends up delivered to and consumed by the end user.

2.2. In reality, three thick layers of filters sift Internet content and efficiently protect us from Internet rubbish: personal settings, the Viral Editor, and relevance algorithms.

2.2.1. **Personal settings**: by adding a bookmark or a friend, a user claims digital territory and makes it a home place with familiar routes and people. Since these routes and people have been personally picked and tested, they form highly reliable digital surroundings for each of us.

2.2.2. **The Viral Editor**[1] is a distributed entity of the Internet, a sort of artificial intelligence whose "processing chips" are people – users.

[1] The concept of the Viral Editor was developed in *Human as media. The emancipation of authorship*. (2014).

2.2.2.1. If a user sees something noteworthy, he or she shares it in the hope of eliciting a response, the currency of social capital. If others find it interesting, they share, too, and viral distribution begins.

2.2.2.2. In the process, all participants decide what to select, add, and remove and how to comment, illustrate and enhance. They all micro-edit content on the fly during viral distribution – hence the Viral Editor.

2.2.2.3. The Viral Editor not only handles the selection, framing, and distribution but also serves as an ongoing referendum on significance. Through comments, likes, and reposts, people vote on the importance of content, creating the largest machine of direct democracy in history.

2.2.2.4. The Viral Editor turns the noteworthy for one into the newsworthy for many and kills journalism. It recruits all the expertise, evidence, and wit that people possess, as they all compete for recognition while sharing.

2.2.2.5. For every user, the network of digital friends consists of people with close social demographics and tastes. This ensures the high relevance of their information exchange. The Viral Editor delivers content precisely to whom it may concern.

2.2.2.6. In the blogosphere, the Viral Editor was an algorithm of relevance made up of humans. It was slow and considerate. Social media introduced digital algorithms of relevance and turned the Viral Editor into the Viral Inquisitor.

2.2.3. **Algorithms of relevance** analyze a user's past clicks to determine what content a user will be exposed to in the future. A user ends up in the prison of past preferences, but the convenience provided by this prison is enormous: it tailors content to our interests.

2.3. Personal bookmarks, the network of friends acting as the Viral Editor, and algorithms of relevance sift out 99.999...% of Internet noise and deliver content with personal customization unimaginable in any medium of any epoch.

2.4. Everything you need for efficient digital media literacy is already here. The only missing piece is you.

2.5. Media literacy is the hygiene of clicks. The hygiene of clicks means picking links, bookmarks, and digital friends appropriately and with the awareness of consequences.

2.6. Digital media are designed to do an incredible job for you, with one purpose – to suck you in and keep you within. This, not any wrong or malicious content, is the major danger posed by digital media.

3. Media literacy is authorship management

3.1 The Internet emancipated authorship.[1] In the entire history before the Internet, humankind had approximately 300 million authors – people capable of expressing their thoughts or reactions beyond their physical reach. Now, in just 40 years, we have five billion authors.

3.2. Everybody has gotten the technical capacity of authorship, but not all users have meaningful content to share. On average, 1% of users post, 9% comment, and 90% like, repost, or simply scroll and pause.

3.3. As an emancipated author, people may consistently or sporadically fall into one of the following categories of heavy or lazy authors.

3.3.1. **Clicking authors:** their non-verbal activity includes liking, reposting, clicking links, or pausing while scrolling. These are still "authorial" and somewhat meaningful choices that define the significance of content and the speed of its distribution.

3.3.2. **Interjectional authors:** they contribute emotional affirmation through interjections (WOW, LOL, OMG) and their digital surrogates – emojis, gifs, memes, and such. The level of

---

[1] The concept of the emancipation of authorship was developed in *Human as media. The emancipation of authorship*. (2014).

exposure is higher, so they can count on a response (likes) to their activity from others.

3.3.3. **Commenting authors:** they produce the major portion of user-generated content and contribute an agonistic mentality, thus increasing drama and engagement for all.

3.3.4. **Principal authors:** they possess sufficient charisma and (sometimes) expertise to start discussions or even discourses.

3.4. The heavy authors (commenting and principal) contribute content. The lazy authors (clicking and interjectional) contribute engagement and keep the machine rolling.

3.5. In different situations and moods, a user can act as either a heavy or lazy author. The higher the activity, the more exposure, the more social capital, and the more hate a user can harvest.

3.6. Media literacy assumes the awareness of the spectrum of authorial opportunities, benefits, and risks. By posting, commenting, reposting, or just liking, you decide the level of exposure for gaining both social capital and hate.

3.6.1. Remember: even pausing while scrolling exposes you to the algorithms – and try not to get too paranoid about it.

4. Media literacy is fake management

4.1. All accounts on social media are fakes. In the digital, we all are legitimate con artists.

4.1.1. Tribal life ensured that everyone's behavior was exposed to others for better interaction. Writing withdrew an individual from the collective immersion and exposed ideas, not behavior. Digital media have hybridized those two states.

4.1.2. On social media, users exhibit their behavior to others, but it's no longer the behavior of a real person. This is digital speech-behavior, created by a user for his or her digital persona according to the settings of a social media platform.

4.1.3. In physical reality, our capacities for showing off were quite limited. In writing, creating a character would require outstanding talent. Digital media are directly designed to fabricate our desirable selves in the hope of eliciting a better response.

4.1.4. By allowing our alternative and presumably better digital selves, social media fulfill the highest need in Maslow's pyramid – self-actualization. The thirst for response that fuels social media is the Hegelian struggle for recognition, digitally refined and amplified.

4.1.5. Everyone does it; some do it skillfully by faking also news and other activities with the same purpose – for better response and subsequent gains. Making others believe in the induced reality is the defining feature of induced reality. Digital reality is entirely induced.

4.2. In physical reality, truths were verified by collisions with solid objects. In digital reality, the only solid objects are others and algorithms. Truth is everything that complies with others and algorithms.

4.3. Digital media literacy is the competence of faking self appropriately and the awareness of others faking themselves. Digital media literacy is well-measured fake tolerance.

4.4. The further development of digital media, with textual generative AI, visual generative AI, and, soon, behavioral generative AI, will only extend these marvellous digital capacities of remodelling the self and its habitat.

4.5. Fake accounts or fake news are not the issue – beware of addiction, polarization, and addiction to polarization.

5. Media literacy is hormone therapy

5.1. Digital consumption is a hormone-driven activity. Smartphones and digital platforms exploit hormonal stimuli developed in humans by evolution.

5.1.1. Curiosity is a beneficial trait because it increases the chances for finding food and shelter or mating. Socialization is a beneficial strategy because it improves interaction and tribal integrity for survival and procreation.

5.1.2. Nature rewards curiosity and socialization with cocktails of dopamine, serotonin, and other pleasure-inducing hormones. Digital media have learned to exploit these survival mechanisms, making users digital hunter-gatherers, united in virtual tribes.

5.2. These hormonal stimuli are tiny; they are barely sensed. Unlike the strong hormonal rewards for sex and eating, which aim for completion and result in satiation, the rewards for curiosity and socialization aim to maintain certain behavioral activity, not to complete it.

5.3. Unlike physical reality, where curiosity and socialization required effort, all it takes in digital reality is scrolling and clicking. Sensing quasi-pleasure but never satiation, we spend more and more time online. In digital media, this is a feature, not a bug.

5.3.1. This is where digital addiction comes from. It's not even pleasure itself but the yearning to experience that fleeting pleasure again that drives people check their devices in the hope to see a like or to find and share something valuable, potentially leading to a response.

5.4. Media literacy implies the awareness of the hormonal nature of digital consumption. Neither withdrawal nor self-shaming are solutions, but recognition, acceptance, and balancing. Reasonable people can recognize and cope with guilty pleasures; this is simply another one.

5.4.1. The best way of not doing something is doing something else, preferably with a similar degree of excitement. It is hard to resist digital seduction, but there is a chance to employ other activities so that they compete for your time with digital devices.

5.5. "Dopamine culture" is on the rise. The hormonal nature of digital consumption needs to be taken into account when exploring digital business opportunities, assessing digital threats to a healthy lifestyle, or searching for solutions to digital addiction.

6. Media literacy is prompt literacy

6.1. Focusing on answers was the Stone Age of the Internet. Now the platforms want to know questions, and they are getting better at it. Despite humans still mocking algorithms for stupid guesses, the latter can predict our impulsive or hidden desires with remarkable accuracy.

6.2. Either you know what you want from the media environment, or the media environment will make you want what it wants you to want. This is fine as long as you are aware of it: shaping your wants is one of the greatest services of digital media.

6.2.1. The disservice of guessing users' wants is that the platform algorithms take over users' lives. In the digital world, platform convenience enslaves.

6.3. Similar to psychoanalysis, the realization of your digital needs, whatever they may be, helps you acquire awareness of them and regain control over them.

6.4. The issue of control over queries has grown with the arrival of generative AI. Answers already belong to various digital entities – databases, search engines, relevance algorithms, and generative AIs – while holding onto control over queries remains one of the last human prerogatives.

6.5. With the rise of generative AI that handles various human activities, prompt literacy is becoming the fundamental aspect of digital media literacy.

6.5.1. After integrating AI with the Internet of Things and smart homes, prompt literacy will become the key not only to convenience but also to physical safety and survival.

6.5.1.1. Everyone will have to be prompt-proficient with virtual assistants, smart cars, and smart homes so that they do not make one bankrupt, ruin careers and personal lives through digital hallucinations or misinterpretations, or, worse, kill their users.

7. Media literacy is social engineering

7.1. The awareness of media effects results in the mindfulness of media use. When using media as tools and interfaces, one needs to be cognizant of their environmental – cognitive and cultural – effects as well as their services and disservices.

7.2. This knowledge can be used proactively to maximize the services and minimize the disservices of media. More beneficial and less harmful media use can be engineered at the individual level (for oneself) and, with some reservations, even at the collective level (for others).

7.3. Media engineering means cultivating, in various practices and habits, the essential effects of literacy: linearity, sequentiality, scheduling, cataloging, deliberation, long immersive reading, isolated agency, rational detachment, delayed response, delayed gratification, etc.

7.3.1. For example, learn to give yourself (or your children) extra rewards for activities with longer efforts and delayed gratification. Find some other pleasure of fulfillment that can beat, at the hormonal level, the instant but minuscule gratification of digital media use.

7.3.2. Keep cataloguing things, put ideas or events onto mind maps or timelines, use short-, mid-, and long-term planning, postpone your responses (when applicable), use diverse forms of digital and offline socialization.

7.3.3. The ideal tool of media literacy for the digital era was invented long ago. It is the book. Read books. There is simply no better and more natural catalyst for all the effects of literacy we regret losing than long reading.

7.3.3.1. Crucially important: reading must be lengthy enough to induce detachment from immediate reality and immersion in what is being read. Find genres that can keep you reading without distraction for at least an hour (the max length of a TV series episode).

8. Media literacy is time management

8.1. Traditional media literacy programs inherited from classical education the ethos of teaching ***how to do***. This makes sense when you deal with an instrument; however, when media are the environment, media literacy should be anti-environmental – it should teach ***how not to do***.

8.1.1. No one teaches a person how to breathe – it comes naturally from environmental adaptation. But some practices of regaining control over the body teach how not to breathe (such as yoga or tai chi, for example).

8.1.2. The instrumental use of digital media no longer needs to be learned. Media designers have ensured that you will master the necessary skills on the fly. But not using devices when everyone else does requires some spiritual guidance or even enforcement.

8.2. Media literacy is about comprehending, appreciating, and withstanding the environmental power of media.

8.3. Media literacy is the skill and discipline of switching between media and, ultimately, of willingly turning off any medium, no matter how emotionally attractive and sensory pleasing this medium may be.

8.4. In the digital environment, media literacy is not about how to use media; media literacy is about how not to use media.

8.5. Digital media literacy is the discipline of resisting the instant reward for tiny effort and enjoying the delayed gratification for significant effort.

8.6. Digital media literacy is life (time) management.

<u>Other books by Andrey Mir (available on Amazon)</u>

Human as Media. The Emancipation of Authorship. (2014).

"With its concept of the 'viral editor' (now transformed, in our harsher decade, into 'viral inquisitor'), 'Human as Media' remains mandatory reading for anyone wishing to understand the disruptions of the digital."

– Martin Gurri, author of "The Revolt of the Public."

Postjournalism and the Death of Newspapers. The Media after Trump: Manufacturing Anger and Polarization. (2020).

"As Mir argues, this change in the economic structure of the news media has quietly transformed journalism from a theoretically neutral means of "manufacturing consent" into a political cause that people are rallied into supporting, usually by inciting them to some form of outrage."

– Murtaza Hussain, "The Intercept".

Digital Future in the Rearview Mirror: Jaspers' Axial Age and Logan's Alphabet Effect (2024).

"Has anyone else writing today about the Internet and the new media it's spawned, come off sounding as much like McLuhan on steroids?... 'Digital Future in the Rearview Mirror' is sure to become a cornerstone of media ecology literature. At epic length, in a narrative that has been assembled with phenomenal detail, Mir examines how 'the contours of the digital future resemble patterns from the tribal past'."

– William Kuhns, co-editor of The Book of Probes (with Eric McLuhan and David Carson).

Made in the USA
Monee, IL
04 November 2026

67384342R00105